The West Side Carbondale, Pennsylvania Mine Fire

The West Side Carbondale, Pennsylvania Mine Fire

Kathleen Purcell Munley

University of Scranton Press

Scranton and London

Library of Congress Cataloging-in-Publication Data

Munley, Kathleen Purcell.
The West Side Carbondale, Pennsylvania mine fire / Kathleen Purcell Munley.
p. cm.
Includes bibliographical references.
ISBN 978-1-58966-212-4 (pbk.)
1. Mine fires--Pennsylvania--Carbondale--History--20th century. 2. Mine fires--Social aspects--Pennsylvania--Carbondale--History--20th century. 3. West Side (Carbondale, Pa.)--History--20th century. 4. Carbondale (Pa.)--History--20th century. 5. West Side (Carbondale, Pa.)--Social conditions--20th century. 6. Carbondale (Pa.)--Social conditions--20th century. 7. West Side (Carbondale, Pa.)--Biography. 8. Carbondale (Pa.)--History--Biography. 9. Interviews--Pennsylvania--Carbondale. I. Title.
TN315.M8 2010
363.37'9--dc22

2010041837

Distribution:
University of Scranton Press
Chicago Distribution Center
11030 S. Langley Chicago, IL 60628

PRINTED IN THE UNITED STATES OF AMERICA

Dedication

This work is dedicated to the people of Carbondale's West Side and in particular, to those who lived in the mine fire zone and whose lives were forever altered by their experiences during this difficult period in Carbondale's history.

CONTENTS

Introduction

A 1957 article in *Pageant* magazine called it the "town on a hot seat."[1] Mine fires were nothing new in Pennsylvania, but the one that had been burning under Carbondale, Pennsylvania, for more than a decade was especially ominous—and deadly.

Years of expensive efforts to extinguish the fire had been worse than futile; some experts thought they had actually propelled the fire's spread. Now the fire which had been initially little more than a curiosity—grass growing in winter where the heat from below had melted the snow—and then a nuisance, and then a danger to just one section of the city, had become a mortal threat to a proud old city. It looked like Carbondale, a city that had lived and prospered by anthracite coal, was going to die by it.

Carbondale was a pleasant and apparently still thriving small city of just over 16,000 people in the late 1950s. Though badly hit by the decline of the Pennsylvania anthracite industry that had begun in the 1920s, Carbondale still boasted a flourishing business district, many manufacturing companies, two high schools, and numerous churches, parks, and playgrounds. Like most American cities and towns at that time, it was made up of neighborhoods—blue-collar to well-off professional—that mostly still kept distinct religious and ethnic identities. Its western most region—known as the West Side—was home to working-class families of Italian, Irish, and Eastern-European descent, many of whom had lived there for generations. It was they who ultimately suffered the most from the fire that spread beneath their homes.

The interviews with Carbondale residents that form the core of this book reveal that the initial awareness of the presence of the fire grew slowly in the late 1940s. At first, it was no cause for alarm for anyone who did not live near the garbage dump where careless dumping and burning of trash had ignited a coal seam lying close to the surface. The smoke, steam, and smell seemed confined to a small area for several years. But in November 1952, an elderly couple whose modest house was several blocks from the dump were found dead in their bed, asphyxiated by carbon monoxide from the fire which had spread to a point beneath their home. Suddenly, the deadly threat was very real.

West Siders soon found themselves living with fear and anxiety, as well as sagging houses, smoldering sinkholes, and mine inspectors with carbon monoxide detectors visiting their houses at all hours of the day and night. The city first attempted to deal with the fire by itself, with only the sometimes half-hearted cooperation of the Hudson Coal Company, in whose abandoned mine the fire had started. Expensive attempts to flush the fire with water, to seal it off from air, or to damp it down with fireproof materials all failed. By the time the writer from *Pageant* came to town, it was clear that digging the fire out was the only solution.

But excavation was not only dauntingly costly; it promised to destroy the entire West Side—one-third of the city. Digging the fire out of this large area would entail taking hundreds of homes and other properties. Most of the West Side would be destroyed, and West Siders would have to be compensated for their properties—and relocated.

Carbondale's mine fire established something of a precedent for confronting mine fires. Years of costly failures to eradicate the fire by conventional methods made it clear that the surest way of eliminating the threat to the whole city was to dig the burning coal out. A dig-out in itself was not a new concept, but excavating a fire of this size—approximately 120 acres on the surface, and a hundred feet or more down—had never been attempted.

In the end, Carbondale took on the fire with a massive project involving federal, state, and local governments, the first-of-its-kind cooperative venture in the United States. The "Appalachian Mine Fire Control Project No. 24" was conducted under the Appalachian

Regional Development Act of 1965. Ultimately, the fire was disgorged, but at enormous cost.

The financial toll was in the millions of dollars; the human toll, incalculable. Some one thousand West Side residents were forced to sell their homes and move out of beloved neighborhoods, leaving behind lifetimes of traditions, memories, and dreams. They watched as homes, that in many cases had been built by their own or their ancestors' hands, were knocked or burned down to get on with digging out the fire. Their neighborhoods were completely obliterated. Their trauma was compounded in many cases by the fact that the money they received for their condemned houses was not enough to buy a new house elsewhere. Torn from a community they never thought they would have to leave, many former West Siders can still describe in searing detail how the Carbondale mine fire changed their lives.

This study started as part of a long-range research project on the Carbondale Mine Fire. While it endeavors to identify the causes of the fire and explores efforts to eradicate it, the book is primarily focused on the effects of the fire on the residents of the mine fire area. Many residents of Carbondale have contributed to this book. When I began it in 1998, I sought to make it an oral history. To that end, I interviewed some twenty persons who were directly involved in the mine fire, either as residents of the West Side during the fire, or in the attempts to extinguish it. Some of those interviewed were fairly young during the mine fire years, others were older, and some have passed on since they were interviewed. I also drew on interviews that were conducted by journalists from several national publications who wrote about the fire while it was burning.

Memories of this traumatic experience are an important part of the historical record of the Carbondale mine fire. However, this study illustrates the intricate and complex nature of historical research and interpretive study as I seek to weave together various types of sources in order to more thoroughly investigate one event in time. By combining traditional historical methodology with information gathered from oral interviews, we are able to view the subject through the eyes of the people involved—people whose memories of the events and/or their emotional proximity to those events are often affected in ways that alter or color their understanding of the situation, and may run contrary to official accounts in records and documents. Yet, it is this divergence from the traditionally gathered data that provides the historian with a fuller, more complete and, therefore, more accurate comprehension of the depth and gravity of the consequences of events on people, and, in this case, on a community.

Chapter 1:

Mine Fires

Around the world, there are thousands of underground coal fires burning. The United States, with the world's largest coal reserves, has hundreds. Pennsylvania's sixty-eight known mine fires are the most of any state, *Smithsonian* magazine reported in 2005.[1] Most of them smolder away underground, largely unnoticed. Mine fires are very difficult and extremely costly to fight; those that don't threaten people and property (and some that do, like the fire that has forced the evacuation of Centralia, Pennsylvania) are often simply monitored and left to burn themselves out, a process that may take centuries.

Though most mine fires result from human actions (often human carelessness and stupidity), some have natural causes. Evidence of prehistoric fires, ignited by something other than human hands, has been found. During an investigation of one eastern mine, it was discovered that a fire had taken a strip of coal as much as one hundred feet wide along an outcrop for a distance of about four miles.[2] Investigators, finding no heat or fire in these workings, concluded that this fire had existed in prehistoric times and had been both started and extinguished by natural forces.[3] Lightning, forest fires, and even exothermic bacteria from decaying plants or animals, can ignite surface coal seams. But most fires have a human trigger.

Reverend Charles Beatty, writing in his diary in 1766, referred to a mine fire burning near the top of Mount Washington in Allegheny County, Pennsylvania. He noted, "A fire being made by the workmen not far from the place where they dug the coal, and left burning when they went away, by the small dust communicated itself to the body of the coals and set it on fire, and has now been burning almost a twelve month entirely underground. . . . The earth in some places is so warm, that we could hardly bear to stand upon it; at one place where the smoke came up we opened a hole in the earth till it was hot as to burn paper thrown into it; the steam . . . so strong of sulphur that we could scarce bear it. . . . The smoke arising out of this mountain appears to be much greater in rainy weather than at any other times."[4] We know that the Mount Washington fire was active as late as 1846, but seems to have burned out later in the nineteenth century.

Two other nineteenth-century fires, one in Perry County, Ohio, and the other in Carbon County, Pennsylvania, reportedly started in active deep mines and extended to the surface as abandoned-mine fires. The efforts, largely futile, to combat both fires, attracted a good deal of attention. The Ohio fire was said to have ignited in 1884 and was still burning in some "isolated areas" in the twentieth century.[5] Work to stop its spread began in 1936 as a Works Progress Administration project.[6] The Pennsylvania fire was reported to have ignited in February 1859 and was contained after many "costly attempts by private parties."[7]

Prior to 1933, the Federal Bureau of Mines was a sort of clearing house for investigations of mine fires and advice for local authorities and mine owners on methods to control them. During the New Deal era of the 1930s, mine fire control and removal in abandoned mines was undertaken by a number of federal agencies, including the Civil Works Administration (CWA) and the Works Progress Administration (WPA). Federal mining engineers of the Federal Bureau of Mines routinely worked as consultants to these various federal agencies on mine fire projects.

As time went on, the federal government became the primary agency for dealing with mine fires anywhere in the United States. The 1949 Department of the Interior Appropriations Acts for 1949–55 contained provisions that authorized the Federal Bureau of Mines to conduct a program for control and extinguishing of mine fires in inactive coal deposits.[8] At the same time—through into the 1950s—the federal government became increasingly involved in coal-mine inspections, targeting potential hazards and making various recommendations designed to control or eliminate hazards. Federal funding for mine fire control and extinguishing became available at that time.

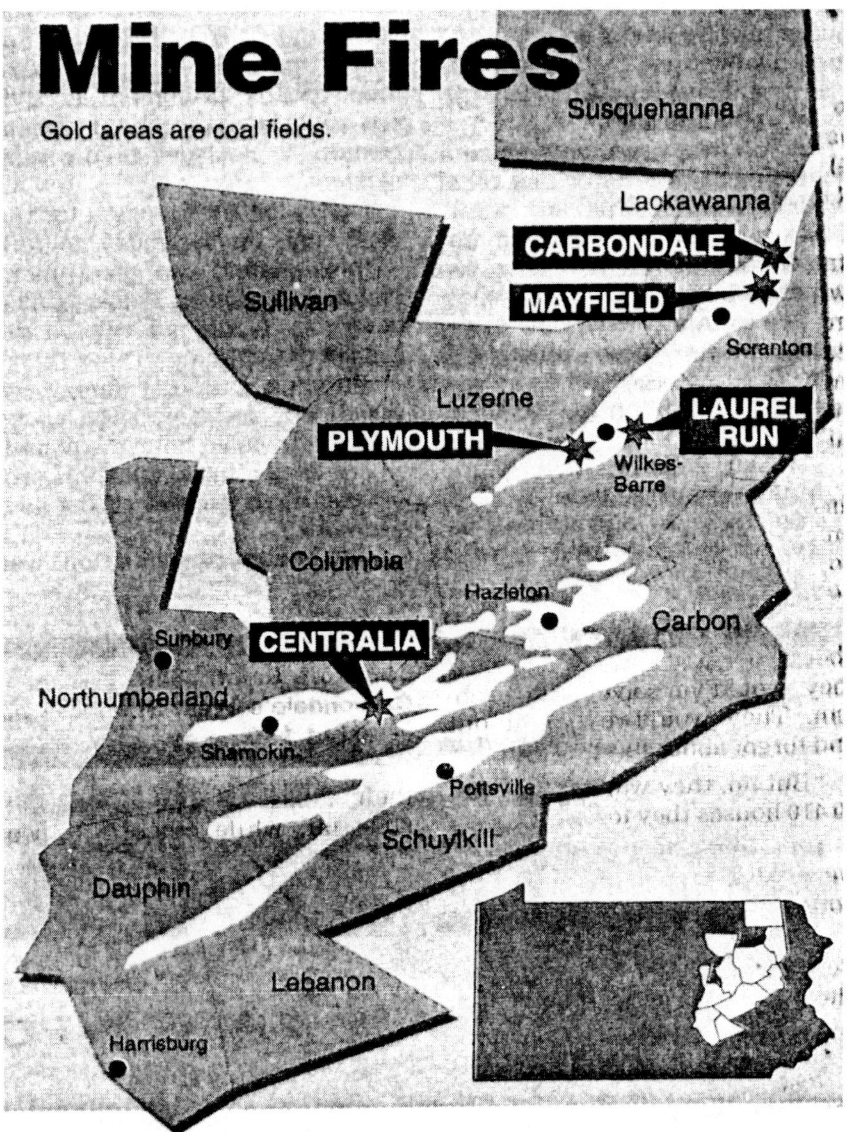

"Mine Fires" - *The Sunday Times*, February 23, 1997, A10

How Mine Fires Start

Mine fires occur in either of two situations: in inactive coal formations that may involve partly mined coal, and in unmined coal formations.[9] Those located in inactive mines with partly mined coal are considered by mining experts to be the more serious because they burn rapidly and spread, often extending over large areas. Fires in unmined coal are a different sort of problem and are most often found in the western part of the United States.

Fires in active mines are usually attacked immediately and quickly controlled.[10] Though the means to extinguish the blaze may leave the mine inaccessible to miners for an extended period after the fire is out, these kinds of mine fires seldom affect the surface or the people living nearby.[11]

Fires in abandoned mines, however, present all sorts of problems. The first is that they usually go undetected for a long time. Often, they have spread to encompass hundreds of acres underground before they are discovered. Obviously, this makes control extremely difficult.[12]

Fires in mined, partly mined, or abandoned mine workings—as was the case with the Carbondale mine fire—can smolder slowly, but typically they burn rapidly. Combustion, of course, depends on the amount of oxygen that comes in contact with the coal. Underground mining contains numerous passageways that allow air to reach the fire. In addition, oxygen passes through the many crevices and sinkholes in the land above the mine (the overburden) that are the inevitable result of mining operations. The more extensive the mining, the more difficult it is to control a mine fire once it has started. Those experienced with mine fire control efforts observe that a fire usually progresses along the "ribs in the roof coal and shales of the abandoned entries."[13] "All mine fire control in the East and in most of the West has been in mined coal deposits."[14]

Igniting a mine fire is disturbingly easy. Coal formations are large areas of combustible fuel. The ignition temperature of coal is between 800 and 900 degrees Fahrenheit, but coal does not have to reach those temperatures to begin to burn. If coal is heated to 200 degrees and oxygen is present, it can catch fire, and, depending on the availability of oxygen, continued oxidation will accelerate and expand the fire in the bed.[15]

There are many sources for ignition of mine fires. Some are natural, and not much can be done to prevent them. For example, forest fires have been known to spread underground by setting surface coal outcrops alight. And the reverse—a mine fire that starts a forest fire—is also not unknown. Writing in *Smithsonian*, Kevin Krajick reported that a century-old mine fire near Glenwood Springs, Colorado, ignited a forest fire that consumed twelve thousand acres and forty-three buildings in the summer of 2002. Putting out the forest fire cost $6.5 million; the underground mine fire is still burning.[16]

Bacterial and chemical reactions have also been identified as causes of ignition. If garbage is dumped on or near a coal outcrop, the heat generated by the decay of the organic matter in the trash can set fire to the flammable material in the dump.[17] Then the dump fire can spread and light the coal. Decaying organic matter in forests can have the same effect, and this is suspected of being the cause of some of the underground fires known to be burning in remote wilderness areas of both the U.S. and Canadian West. Spontaneous combustion is also possible. Some forms of very soft coal, found in "low-rank" beds can ignite spontaneously due to a chemical reaction.[18] These kinds of coal tend to disintegrate easily when exposed to air. However, this type of chemical reaction is not possible in either bituminous or anthracite coal.

Ultimately, human activity—too often, human stupidity—is the most common cause of fires. One of the most common is burning trash or brush near an exposed coal bed. Warming fires, particularly those started by people digging for coal from abandoned mines or by children playing near such areas, have been known to start mine fires. Mine refuse, containing carbonaceous waste materials, stored or placed above coal beds is another source.

How Mining Methods Contribute to Mine Fires

Early mining methods contribute greatly to the spread of

mine fires. Mining was done near an outcrop, and large amounts of coal were often left. The need for drainage, air, and access meant that numerous surface cuts were made. Entrances were narrow, leaving large deposits of coal in place. In order to maintain roof support, coal located at the top of the operation was left untouched. Likewise, due to accumulations of water in the mines, coal was often left unmined on the floors of the chambers. As a result, there is still a great deal of coal in nineteenth- and early twentieth-century mines that were deemed "worked out." Worked-out areas close to outcrops were often connected to deep mines. Altogether, this was a perfect scenario for an underground inferno.

With the decline in the anthracite coal industry of Pennsylvania and the abandonment of large deep-mining operations throughout the anthracite region, the number of mine fires increased. As coal companies shut down, sold out, or otherwise removed themselves from actual production, many coal fields were divided into smaller holdings or simply abandoned. (Many municipalities in the anthracite regions found themselves the owners of mines they had seized for tax delinquencies, but large tracts of land in the coal regions had no owner of record by the 1960s.) By the mid 1960s, strip mining—unsightly and environmentally disastrous—was the major form of coal mining that remained.

Among their many other unsavory attributes, strip-mining companies were notorious for digging out all of the reclaimable coal and moving on without backfilling and restoring the strip site. This left ugly abandoned pits, many near cities and towns, which became convenient places for municipalities and people in general to dump and burn garbage. This practice is known to have caused the underground fire that has consumed the Schuylkill County towns of Centralia and the ironically named Byrnesville, and is almost surely what triggered the fire under Carbondale.

These easily ignited exposed outcrops spread the fire into the seams and passages of the abandoned mines beneath. As a result, fires often went unnoticed for months or even years. (As explained later in this chapter, detecting the size of an underground fire, or even establishing its existence, is difficult.) It was only when small whiffs of steam or a slight odor of sulfur gave evidence that many fires were even noticed, and then only by the people living nearby. Many subterranean fires have burned for as long as twenty-five years with no surface indication of their presence. As they advance, however, they eat away at the coal pillars that miners leave to support the mine ceiling. As these pillars burn to ash and collapse, the classic manifestations of mine fires present themselves in the form of the subsidence, smoke, dangerous gases, steam, and the smell of sulfur. These are all signs that the people who live on top of the mine fire are in serious trouble.

Not only do mine fires destroy (or at least seriously compromise) the value of property in the area affected, they pose critical threats to the residents' health, safety, and well-being. It is not an exaggeration to say that living over a burning mine is a disaster in the making for everyone.

Unique Features of Underground Fires

Extinguishing a mine fire is difficult, unpredictable, and exorbitantly expensive. Sometimes, it is impossible. The fire under Centralia, for example, is too big to do anything but monitor it and evacuate anyone likely to be affected by it. (As of 2005, Centralia, Pennsylvania, had only twelve tenacious residents remaining.) Experts estimate that the Centralia fire could burn for another 250 years. Residents of other nearby communities hope that ground water, and the fact that coal seams are not necessarily continuous, will protect them from suffering Centralia's terrible fate.[19]

If the Centralia fire does burn into the twenty-third century, it won't come close to being the world's oldest fire. A coal fire at Burning Mountain, Australia, has been burning for 6,000 years; European explorers mistook it for a volcano.[20] But it does illustrate the unique features of an anthracite underground fire which contribute to its potential longevity and the difficulty of putting it out.

Anthracite burns slowly and very hot, because of its low heat conductivity. (These characteristics are what made it a valuable industrial fuel.) The metamorphic rock where anthracite is found, such as slate and gneiss, also has low heat conductivity. As a result, the heat generated by an underground anthracite-fueled fire is not readily absorbed and dissipated through the adjacent geologic material. Thus, it acts like insulation, holding the heat in the area where the coal is burning.[21]

Since subsurface fires burn at a rate equal to the combustible content of the materials, with added factors related to conditions and supply of oxygen, this means that once a fire has become deeply seated, it has the potential of burning for many years, even if the fire area is tightly sealed. By continuously heating at relatively low temperatures, however, dormant fires can become active very quickly due to the condition of the materials in the fire zone. Thus, fires that appear to have been extinguished by flushing can reappear if the area is disturbed and more oxygen becomes available. This is because the flushing probably put out the fire over a large area, but locally the burning materials have become insulated and the fire has kept burning at a low level for a long time. This is called *conditioning*.[22]

Another complicating feature of confronting anthracite mine fires is that anthracite's low heat conductivity results in the production of hydrogen gas. Large amounts can be generated by heating anthracite in the absence of air. Hydrogen can accumulate in the opening above an active mine fire zone, and the repeated burning process can send fires over long distances through openings in subsurface areas.

In addition, anthracite absorbs gases, particularly carbon dioxide—another factor in the persistence and expansion of mine fires. This being the case, it may absorb some of the fumes from the fire areas with the result that air currents tested close to the actual fire may fail to give off detectable combustion gases. Fire fumes and gases cool as they rise from the ground, making it difficult to detect smoke or other indications of a fire.[23]

Fighting the Fire Down Below

There is no single method for controlling or extinguishing a mine fire. Each fire has individual characteristics that determine the best method or combination of methods that have the greatest chance of success. Based on elementary knowledge that all fires require fuel, oxygen, and heat, the formula followed for eradication is removal of the fuel and elimination of the oxygen, or cooling the ignition temperature of the fuel. There are several accepted approaches to accomplish this: excavation, inundation, installation of fire barriers, flushing, and surface sealing. Recently, inert gases and chemicals, usually in the form of foams, have been tried and used.[24]

There are many factors that must be taken into consideration in the technical approach to the fires, but the most important are these: the extent of the fire below the surface or along an outcrop, the threat to the environment, the proximity to populated areas, geological and topographical conditions, and the extent of mining in the zone.[25]

In addition to the technical factors involved in arriving at a plan to confront the fire, there are several other considerations; these include participation of local governments, the effects on the health and well-being of residents, and releases or condemnation proceedings to acquire properties.[26]

Excavation

Excavation is considered generally feasible if it is begun soon after a fire is discovered. This method involves removing the burning material. Accurately locating the fire's boundaries is usually essential if this method is to be economically practical. The extent of the fire will determine if evacuation can safely stay ahead of it. (Mapping the boundaries can be done by methods as low-tech as watching where the snow melts, as technical as infra-red surveying, and as high-tech as satellite imaging. It remains an inexact science, however.)[27] Other factors that must be taken into consideration in deciding to use this method are the availability of a disposal site for the material removed, the nature of the overburden, a sufficient supply of water, and the existence of surface improvements. Recovery of the coal may compensate for the cost of this method of mine fire control.[28]

Inundation

Inundation involves flooding the underground fire with water to lower the temperature of the burning material. Two technologies are used in this approach: flooding and continuous pumping of water. The former method is considered dangerous, costly and difficult to execute. Continuous pumping from the surface into the mine fire has limited appeal, as well. The expense, the large amount of water required, the length of time involved, and the possibility that the water will miss the actual fire all combine to make this a less than satisfactory method of control. "Historically," according to Michael Korb, "many fires in active mines were handled this way; in inactive mines, generally there is little control over the water levels in the mines."[29]

Flushing

Flushing involves filling the holes in the underground fire with fine, noncombustible materials. This is done by injecting a flow of water and these materials into the spaces through boreholes. The injected material is supposed to fill the mine voids and interstices in the surrounding areas, sealing off the spaces through which air can feed the fire.[30]

Experts believe that flushing can be effective if the injected materials can be specifically directed to areas below the surface in such a way that a complete seal can be put in place. The drawback to this method is that it is difficult to create an adequate seal. Frequently, interstices and crevices in the underground areas are not reached and go unfilled. It is nearly impossible to establish a thorough seal in certain areas due to variations in the subsurface areas. Additionally, gravity naturally carries the flushed material downward; even if a complete seal is achieved, gravity can eventually result in its becoming dislodged or compromised. Seals also break if the material dries out and shrinks over time.[31]

In the 1970s, a modification to the flushing procedure was introduced that involves the use of air to inject or blow noncombustible materials into the subsurface mine holes. This process was sometimes called "pneumatic injection."[32] Reported on favorably by mining engineers, this technique was seen as usually decreasing the amount of runoff of noncombustibles in the underground holes. The drawback to this innovation, however, was the fact that it added oxygen to the underground fire zones, thus increasing the potential for the fire to spread or break out somewhere else. To avoid this possibility, scientists working on the problem determined that this likelihood could be eliminated by the use of inert gases rather than air in the injection process.[33]

Barriers and Surface Sealing

Yet another method for fighting mine fires is the building of noncombustible fire barriers. This method essentially involves constructing a dam between the fire and the coal that acts as a barrier and breaks up the line of coal and other combustible materials. Barriers can be trenches, tunnels, or plugs, but whatever the form, the effectiveness of a barrier relies on its being wide enough to prevent the heat of the fire on one side from transferring to the coal on the other side.[34]

Surface sealing is attractive because it is a relatively inexpensive procedure, but it is not easily accomplished. To cut off the fire's air supply, a dense pack of noncombustible material from eight to ten feet thick must be built to completely seal the fire area. The seal must be maintained at this thickness over several years. This allows for the slow dissipation of the fire's heat. If this method is employed successfully, the fire is smothered and the temperature is lowered to a point where the continuation of the fire is impossible.[35]

Mine fire experts believe that the two most effective methods of extinguishing a fire are inundation, if applied correctly, and excavation. Flushing and sealing have proven effective primarily in retarding and controlling the spread of fires. Studies clearly point to the fact that complete excavation of the fire has the highest probability of success.[36]

The Invisible Killer: Carbon Monoxide

Truly terrifying tales of fiery holes opening up and nearly swallowing people or pets have been recounted by witnesses of many fires. But the chief danger to the people living above underground coal fires is the hazardous combustion gases that seep into houses and buildings through cracks in the surface. These dangerous gases can accumulate in closed, unventilated areas such as basements.

Carbon monoxide (CO) is colorless and odorless and is the most serious physical hazard for people living in proximity to a mine fire. It readily combines with hemoglobin in the blood, replacing the oxygen normally carried by it; the results are a wide range of physical symptoms that end in death if the victim is not removed from the source of the gas and treated. Depending on the concentration level of the gas, exposure can result in slight to severe headaches, dizziness, faintness, nausea, and vomiting. High levels of concentration cause collapse, coma, and convulsions, and can lead to life-threatening respiratory failure and death. Michael Korb, an environmental expert, notes that "a concentration of as little as 0.04% (400 parts per million) carbon monoxide in the air can be fatal."[37]

Carbon monoxide is the element most feared by miners, because it can incapacitate and kill in only a few minutes. Indeed, it was the carbon-monoxide-poisoning deaths of Patrick and Elizabeth Collins—killed in the apparent safety of their own bedroom—which alerted the residents of the West Side, and all of Carbondale, to the deadly danger spreading beneath them.

CHAPTER 2:

CARBONDALE, THE PIONEER CITY

Located in the northeastern sector of the Commonwealth of Pennsylvania in Lackawanna County, the last county to be established by the Pennsylvania Assembly, about sixteen miles northeast of Scranton, the county's principal city and county seat, Carbondale was the first place in the United States where, in 1831, an underground coal mine was opened.

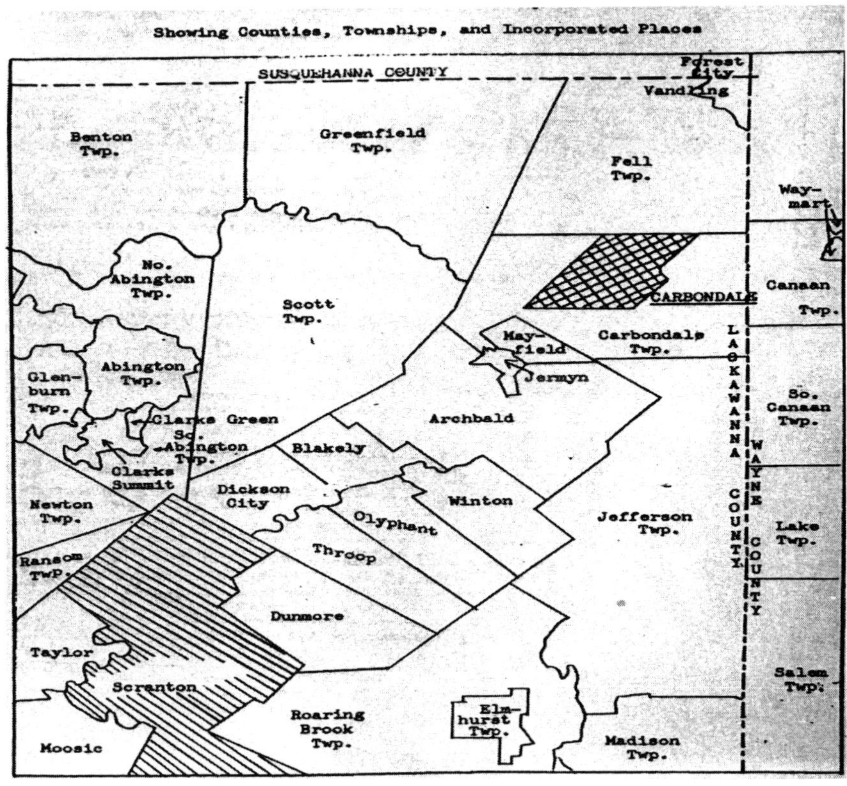

"CARBONDALE AND VICINITY" - *LOCAL GOVERNMENT FINANCIAL STATISTICS*, 1960, RELEASE NO. 38, PENNSYLVANIA DEPARTMENT OF COMMUNITY AFFAIRS, HARRISBURG, PA 1962

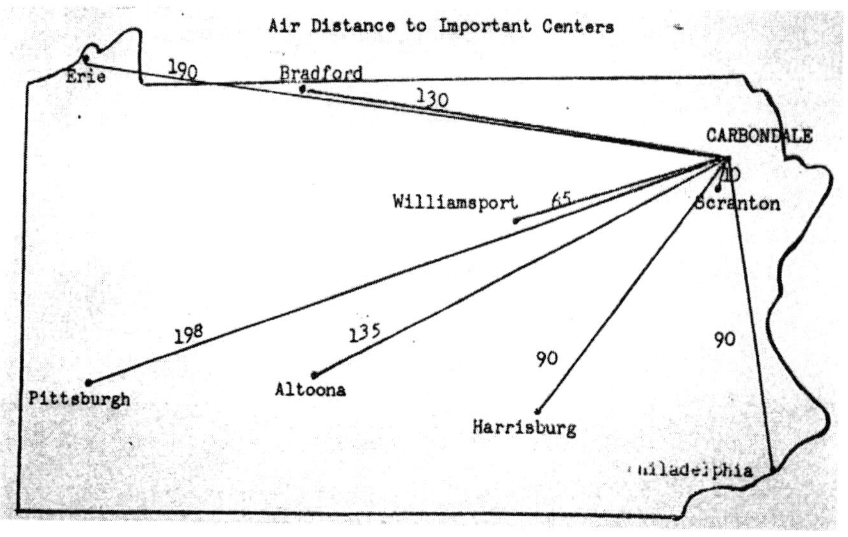

"Carbondale Distances" – History of Carbondale, by A.E. Warne and Helen M. Pierce, Bureau of Business Administration, Pennsylvania State University, March, 1957

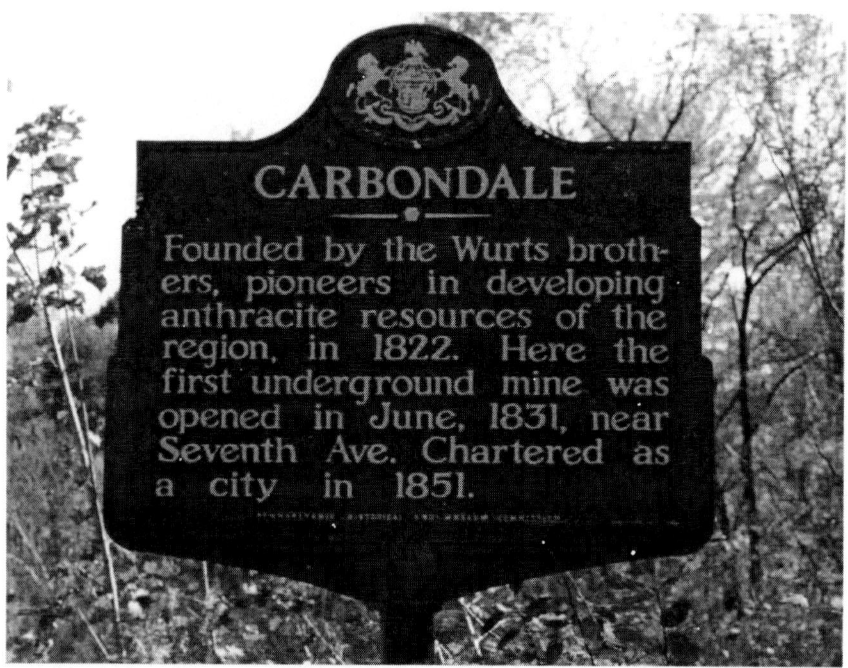

"Plaque in Carbondale Commemorating Development of Anthracite Coal Industry and Chartering of City" – Courtesy of Carbondale Historical Society

The history of this part of Pennsylvania parallels the development of the anthracite coal industry elsewhere in northeastern Pennsylvania. Originally, in the 1700s, New Englanders began migrating into the region around the Lackawanna River in search of good farmlands.[1] This influx of "Yankees" aroused some concern among Pennsylvanians, so in 1786, the Pennsylvania Assembly added the area to the newly created Luzerne County. It remained essentially rural in nature—except for some iron forges along the Lackawanna River—until the turn of the century, when merchant-speculators from Philadelphia to New York began exploring the Valley as a possible area for lucrative investment in coal mining.

Anthracite coal mining was first undertaken on an experimental scale in 1812 at the site of the present-day city of Carbondale. The city, named for the "dale where carbon was formed," came into existence in the early 1830s.[2] The year 1802 is often given as the date of the first settlement.[3] Earlier, farmers had built log cabins along the Lackawanna in this area. In 1814, two brothers, William and Maurice Wurts, engineers from Philadelphia, started searching for coal there. An old Indian legend told of "black mountains" in the region and the Wurts brothers, thinking this might be coal, secured capital from New York City investors and organized a mining company.[4] It took four years for their efforts to be rewarded, but in the spring of 1818, anthracite was discovered in the region known as Ragged Island and later called Barrendale.[5]

The city may be one of the few actual communities to be named by a writer of fiction. Carbondale owes its bucolic-sounding name to Washington Irving. Irving was a friend of one of the Wurts brothers' investors, the New York financier and political leader Philip Hone, and is said to have suggested the name while viewing an exhibit of Ragged Island anthracite in New York City in 1820.[6]

In the years following the War of 1812, American investors became avidly interested in putting their money into anthracite exploration in northeastern Pennsylvania. Coal in general was beginning to show its potential both as home heat and as fuel for iron foundry furnaces, which up to that time were fired by increasingly rare and expensive charcoal. In 1808, a leading resident of Wilkes-

Barre, Judge Jesse Fell (the namesake of Fell Township and the now-lost Fell House Hotel in Wilkes-Barre), showed that anthracite burned hot and clean if it was placed in a grate over an updraft of air. This opened up great possibilities for coal-burning stoves.[7] Josiah White and Erskine Hazard began experiments with anthracite in their wire rope factory in Philadelphia during the War of 1812, when the British Navy's blockade cut them off from shipments of soft coal from Virginia and England. Their results so thoroughly convinced them of anthracite's potential that they purchased huge tracts of land in Carbon County, and in the years from1826 to 1829, they built the Lehigh Coal and Navigation Canal to bring their coal to market in Philadelphia.

At first, the enterprising Wurts brothers tried to use wagons to get the coal to markets outside the Carbondale area. Then they attempted to float the coal on rafts down the Lackawanna River. Both of these methods proved unsatisfactory. Eventually, inspired by the canal-building mania that was sweeping the country, the Wurts brothers decided to build a canal that would connect the Delaware River to the Hudson River. This would open up markets for their coal in New York City and beyond. The Delaware and Hudson Canal took two years to build, and when it was completed in 1828, it connected Honesdale, Pennsylvania, on the Delaware River, with Kingston, New York, on the Hudson.

One problem remained unsolved, however. Between Carbondale and Honesdale stood Moosic Mountain, which tops out at more than 2,200 feet above sea level. But the Wurts brothers were not going to let a mere mountain stand in the way of advancing their enterprise. By 1829, they had built a gravity-driven railroad system that hoisted coal-filled cars from Carbondale up and over the mountain using a complicated set of pulleys. That year the Delaware and Hudson Canal Company shipped seven thousand tons of coal over the Gravity Railroad to the canal at Honesdale.[8] Today, a small city park at the intersection of Belmont and Canaan Streets in Carbondale commemorates the site of the beginning of the Delaware and Hudson Canal Company Gravity Railroad plane. Two years later, anthracite mining moved underground, and a concrete monument commemorating that fact stands on West Seventh Avenue in Carbondale.

The anthracite coal industry took off, and Carbondale grew steadily thereafter. The Delaware and Hudson Canal Company controlled the mines in Carbondale and the entire Lackawanna Valley. Successful mining stimulated further investment and settlement, and within twenty years, the Lackawanna Valley became the most densely populated area in northern Luzerne County.[9] As time passed, success in coal mining spurred the building of several railroads that shipped coal to markets all over America and beyond. These industries, in turn, stimulated the development of many businesses that contributed to the growth of Carbondale and the region, resulting in its designation by the state as the Northern Anthracite Coal Field, an area about fifty-five miles long and five miles wide along the Lackawanna River extending across Lackawanna and Luzerne Counties.[10]

The original settlement of Carbondale was leveled by a fire in 1850, but was rebuilt. In 1851, Carbondale was chartered as a third-class city.[11] The residents sought this official status for their community in part because it would enable them to establish a more secure fire protection plan. Soon, prosperous and thriving, with a solid economic base in coal mining, Carbondale became known as the Pioneer City, a testament to the fact that it was the earliest settlement in the area and the site of the first underground coal mine.

Population Growth and Immigration

Industrial development of Carbondale and the surrounding area created a demand for cheap labor that attracted additional English and Welsh settlers to the region. The ethno-cultural makeup of the area remained essentially unchanged until the 1840s when a large influx of Irish and Germans came looking for work in the coal mines and railroad shops—or seeking opportunities in small businesses. The Irish in particular populated Carbondale. The area went through further ethno-cultural diversification in the years following the American Civil War as thousands of eastern, central, and southern European immigrants began appearing in the coal fields.

Carbondale and its larger neighbor, Scranton, chartered in 1866, as well as the numerous towns that sprang up throughout the Lackawanna Valley, created a locus of regional interest and economic influence which stimulated support for the creation of a separate county. Industrial development coupled with population increase in this northern section of Luzerne County was undeniable, and in 1878, after a referendum in the Lackawanna area in favor of separation, the Pennsylvania Assembly created Lackawanna County, the sixty-seventh and last county to become part of the Commonwealth. At the time of its creation, Lackawanna County boasted a population of 89,269, a number that would more than double in the next twenty years.[12]

Built around mining and other allied industries, including railroads, Carbondale, like the towns that surrounded it, enjoyed about eighty years of prosperity. Ultimately, the dependence of this region on mining was its undoing. The demand for anthracite coal began to decline in the 1920s. Mines in and around Carbondale began closing, railroads serving the community—in particular the Delaware and Hudson and the Ontario and Western—cut back their operations, and businesses both directly and indirectly related to the mining industry shut down or reduced their offices and staffs. Although the region maintained a strong faith in the future of coal mining, the decline continued through the 1930s and 1940s. Strip mining—cheaper but environmentally disastrous—began to replace deep mining.

Fortunately, however, the region developed what state analysts considered a solid base of manufacturing, which exceeded the value of anthracite production by the 1940s.[13] This was very fortunate because Commonwealth studies estimated that Lackawanna County's coal reserves would be largely depleted in fifteen years if the 1922–1944 average rate of extraction continued (see Chart I).[14]

Even the World-War-II years saw no increase in anthracite production, and Lackawanna County showed the greatest proportionate decline of any of the anthracite-producing counties. In the 1950s, the railroads serving Carbondale and other communities in Lackawanna County changed to the more economical diesel fuel. In Carbondale, the Delaware and Hudson railroad roundhouse closed and passenger service ceased between Carbondale and Scranton, leaving hundreds of railroad workers without jobs.

Some senior-level engineers and firemen were able to retain their jobs with the D&H Railroad by commuting to Wilkes-Barre to work on the railroad there; this adjustment was colloquially known as "working out of Wilkes-Barre." It was fortunate for many families that textile production still flourished; that offered work for women and helped sustain family incomes. The major industry and source of work in Carbondale became textiles, an industry which hired mainly female workers.

Thousands of families were impacted by layoffs in the industries built around coal mining, and even with work available in textile mills, many Carbondalians—especially young people—began moving away for jobs. This was especially true following World War II. As many returning veterans failed to find jobs after they returned to civilian life, they began to move to neighboring states, such as New York, New Jersey, and Connecticut where work in manufacturing was readily available (see Charts II and III).

The Pioneer City, like the entire northeastern Pennsylvania region, slowly but steadily declined into worsening economic distress. What the citizens of Carbondale—wearied by war and battered by job losses—did not know was that a new horror was already growing beneath them.[15]

"A View of the D and H Railroad Station off Seventh Avenue" – Courtesy of Carbondale Historical Society

"D and H Railroad Yards" –
Courtesy of Carbondale Historical Society

"Downtown Carbondale circa 1900" –
Courtesy of Carbondale Historical Society

"Early View of Memorial Park and St Rose Church" –
Courtesy of Carbondale Historical Society

"Historic Downtown Carbondale – Main Street" –
Courtesy of Carbondale Historical Society

"Main Street Carbondale circa 1920-30" –
Courtesy of Carbondale Historical Society

"Scene of Crystal Lake near Carbondale" –
Courtesy of Carbondale Historical Society

"Powderly Colliery in South Side Carbondale" –
Courtesy of Carbondale Historical Society

"U.S. Post Office Building on North Main Street Early 20th Century" – Courtesy of Carbondale Historical Society

"YMCA on North Main Street" – Courtesy of Carbondale Historical Society

CHART I:
ANTHRACITE COAL PRODUCTION
LACKAWANNA COUNTY, PENNSYLVANIA

YEAR	NET TONS	YEAR	NET TONS	YEAR	NET TONS
1922	11,282,880	1934	12,188,000	1946	8,759,222
1923	20,659,520	1935	10,816,000	1947	8,322,624
1924	20,092,800	1936	11,161,000	1948	8,504,311
1925	13,706,560	1937	8,833,000	1949	6,138,728
1926	18,979,520	1938	8,119,000	1950	6,473,588
1927	16,754,080	1939	8,718,000	1951	5,733,782
1928	16,347,520	1940	8,667,000	1952	5,323,145
1929	17,217,760	1941	8,531,000	1953	3,799,331
1930	15,141,000	1942	8,186,790	1954	3,420,744*
1931	12,644,000	1943	8,598,443	1955	2,595,000*
1932	11,569,000	1944	8,688,779		
1933	11,206,000	1945	7,626,734		

* Data from the Pennsylvania Department of Mines. These numbers are not quite the same as those reported by the Federal Bureau of Mines.

Source: The Pennsylvania State University, Historical Statistics of Pennsylvania's Mineral Industries, 1759–1955, March 1957, Table 3, 6–10.

Chart II:

Population Changes 1900–1950

Lackawanna County, Leading Communities, and the State of Pennsylvania

	Lackawanna	Carbondale	Olyphant	Dickson City	Honesdale	Scranton	PA County
1900	193,831	13, 536	6,180	4,948	2,864	102,026	6,302,115
1910	259,570	17,040	8,505	9,331	2,945	129,867	7,665,111
1920	286,311	18,640	10,236	11,049	2,756	137,783	8,720,017
1930	310,397	20,061	10,743	12,395	5,490	143,433	9,631,350
1940	301,243	19,371	9,252	11,548	5,687	140,404	9,900,180
1950	257,396	16,296	7,047	8,948	5,662	125,536	10,498,012

Source: U.S. Department of Commerce, Bureau of Census, 1950 Census of Population, Number of Inhabitants of Pennsylvania, Release No. P-A 38, Advance Reports, Series PC-8, No. 37; and Prior Censuses.

Chart III:

Percentage Change from Previous Census

	Lackawanna	Carbondale	Olyphant	Dickson City	Honesdale	Scranton	PA County
1910	33.0	25.9	37.6	88.6	2.8	27.3	21.6
1920	10.3	9.4	20.4	18.4	6.4	6.1	13.8
1930	8.4	7.6	5.0	12.2	99.2	4.1	10.5
1940	-3.0	-3.4	-13.9	-6.8	3.6	-2.1	2.8
1950	-14.6	-15.9	-23.8	-22.5	-0.4	-10.6	6.0

Source: U.S. Department of Commerce, Bureau of Census, 1950 Census of Population, Number of Inhabitants of Pennsylvania, Release No. P-A 38, Advance Reports, Series PC-8, No. 37; and Prior Censuses.

Carbondale in the 1950s was a pleasant community that basked in its proud, albeit declining industrial and commercial history. It was composed of several distinct neighborhoods, defined essentially by ethnicity and class.

East of the Delaware and Hudson Railroad tracks that bisected the city lay the city's major business area. Carbondale's Main Street is U.S. Route 6, which enters the city from the south and continues eastward from Carbondale to the New York and New Jersey state lines. As in many towns and cities that made fortunes during the nineteenth century, Carbondale's "best" residential neighborhoods were near the business district. This section contained some splendid homes built by Carbondale's industrial, commercial, and professional gentry, most of whom were of English/Scotch/Welsh ancestry, or were upwardly mobile Irish and Italians. Many of Carbondale's Jews, a small but prosperous merchant/professional group, lived there as well. North and south of the city's central business area, along Main, River, and Church Streets, and up and down intersecting avenues were more residential neighborhoods, which, while not so grand, were nonetheless regarded as "nice" middle-class neighborhoods inhabited by a population of ethnically diverse Carbondalians.

"Aerial View of Carbondale" –
Courtesy of Carbondale Historical Society

"A View Looking North Towards St Rose Church on Church Street" – Courtesy of Carbondale Historical Society

"Brooklyn Street Bridge over the Fallbrook Creek" – Courtesy of William J. Connor

"Cannons in Memorial Park Removed for Scrap during WWII" – Courtesy of William J. Connor

"Catholic Youth Center and St Rose High School on Corner of Church Street and Seventh Avenue" –
Courtesy of Carbondale Historical Society

"D and H Roundhouse" –
Courtesy of William J. Connor

"Diesel Engine on the D and H" –
Courtesy of Carbondale Historical Society

"Diesel Engine on the D and H (2)" –
Courtesy of Carbondale Historical Society

"Downtown Carbondale on Parade Day 1950s" –
Courtesy of William J. Connor

"Eighth Avenue Looking Toward Main Street" –
Courtesy of William J. Connor

"Fall Brook Creek in Carbondale" –
Courtesy of Carbondale Historical Society

"First National Bank Building Main Street" – Courtesy of Carbondale Historical Society

"Hotel Anthracite and the Globe Fashion Shop Main Street" – Courtesy of William J. Connor

"Irving Theatre" –
Courtesy of William J. Connor

"Lincoln Avenue and Main Street
Mitchell Hose Company in the Distance" –
Courtesy of William J. Connor

"MAIN STREET CARBONDALE" –
COURTESY OF WILLIAM J. CONNOR

"MAJESTIC THEATRE WITH CASINO DANCE HALL ABOVE" –
COURTESY OF WILLIAM J. CONNOR

"Memorial Park 1950s" –
Courtesy of Carbondale Historical Society

"Newton Lake Park" –
Courtesy of William J. Connor

"NORTH CHURCH STREET AND LINCOLN AVENUE" –
COURTESY OF WILLIAM J. CONNOR

"OLD HENDRIX MANUFACTURING COMPANY" –
COURTESY OF WILLIAM J. CONNOR

"Presbyterian Church and Methodist Church on Church Street" –
Courtesy of Carbondale Historical Society

"Russell Park 1946 – The Pioneer Blues Baseball Team" –
Courtesy of William J. Connor

"South Main Street at Eighth Avenue – McCawleys on the Left" – Courtesy of William J. Connor

West of the D&H tracks lay a sprawling working-class, blue-collar region called the West Side, which reached as far as the mountains—running north to south on the western edge of the Lackawanna Valley—and bordered Fell Township on the north and Childs Township on the south. It was here that the mine fire was discovered in 1946.

Settled during the years of Carbondale's economic development by various ethnic groups, many of whom came as immigrants, this section of Carbondale was home to primarily first-, second-, and third-generation Americans of Italian and Irish ancestry. Adding to the diversity of this section was the fact that, here and there, in lesser numbers, were also people whose ancestors had come from various Eastern European countries. Although West Siders identified proudly with their location, in reality the region was composed of several distinct neighborhoods, mainly distinguished by ethnicity and familial and other relationships

West Side homes, while modest in comparison to those of the more elite East Side, were frequently surrounded by large tracts containing carefully tended lawns that boasted an array of trees and fruit orchards, bushes, flowers, and vegetable gardens. Many homes had outbuildings that had housed chickens and geese, and as late as the 1950s, some West Side residents still kept poultry. A number of yards also had smokehouses and grape arbors.

Not all the houses on the West Side were modest, though. Sprinkled throughout were several large, elegant properties, especially along Brooklyn Street, south along Route 6, and northward to McGary and Scott Streets. These homes were often the property of families who had achieved some degree of financial success in mining or who had entered a white-collar profession (medicine, law, teaching, small business ownership, and the like) or had advanced through politics.

"SEVENTH AVENUE CROSSING – AN ENTRANCE TO THE WEST SIDE" – COURTESY OF WILLIAM J. CONNOR

Carbondale's "suburbs" included Fell Township to the north and Carbondale Township to the south. Near the city, these townships also had distinct communities of diverse working-class populations—mostly of Irish and Eastern European ancestry. Carbondale's North Main Street ran into Belmont Street, which extended into the neighboring Fell Township and beyond to Vandling and to Forest City in Susquehanna County. When Route 6 was constructed in the 1940s, it connected Carbondale (from North Main Street to Canaan street) to the east with the neighboring community of Waymart in Wayne County and beyond that to Honesdale. Southward, via either Brooklyn Street (Route 6) or Pike Street, the city extends to Carbondale Township and then to the neighboring boroughs of Mayfield, Jermyn, and Archbald. Continuing on Route 6 (or following the valley Main Streets) leads to the so-called Mid-Valley region and from there to Scranton, the seat of Lackawanna County.

Carbondale in the 1940s and '50s was proud of its self-contained, independent status as the largest community in northern Lackawanna County and one of two legislatively designated "cities" in Lackawanna County (the other was Scranton). Although it is evident that economic slippage had already begun, the city residents saw mostly a semi-prosperous, pleasant community with all the good things that made it so.

Carbondale's downtown was a well-ordered business area with shops aplenty for its residents and those of neighboring smaller communities. Ladies shopped in several highly regarded stores for the latest apparel for themselves and their children. Men's clothing was not ignored and Carbondale gentlemen enjoyed a wide range of fashion choices at several "men's" shops. Shoe stores dotted the Main Street and side streets while various dry goods could be purchased at J.C. Penney's, Woolworth's, Newberry's, or smaller stores in both the downtown area and in some adjacent areas. Grocery stores were likewise available for shoppers with several large markets, such as A&P, Acme, and Giant, located in the downtown area, and smaller stores in the various neighborhoods throughout the city. The city had many service shops and businesses devoted to home, autos, appliances, and the like.

"Hospital Street in 1938" – Courtesy of William J. Connor

"Scott Street Looking West from the Neutts Residence" – Courtesy of William J. Connor

"The Wilson Elementary School off Brooklyn Street" – Private Collection

"West Side Playground and the Columbus School" – Courtesy of William J. Connor

There were two well-respected high schools, Benjamin Franklin, the public high school, and St. Rose, the Catholic high school, as well as numerous neighborhood public elementary schools and two parochial elementary schools. Carbondale was a city of churches: two Roman Catholic churches, one each for Baptist, Presbyterian, Methodist, Episcopalian, Assembly of God, and Lutheran worship, and a Jewish Synagogue. Citizens availed themselves of the latest news through several newspapers; two were published in the city, *The Carbondale Daily News*, and the weekly *Carbondale Review*. Most people also read *The Scranton Times* and *The Scranton Tribune*, both of which maintained Carbondale offices.

Carbondale residents liked to say that everything they needed they could get "in town," including medical care at two hospitals. The city's medical community enjoyed an excellent reputation, and in those years, its doctors made house calls on ailing patients. For those who needed the services of lawyers, there were several in the town, and banking services were readily available for the community in one of three banks—all locally owned.

When it came to leisure activities and entertainment, Carbondale's residents had numerous choices. There were two motion picture houses, the Majestic, which offered mainly B movies and "cowboy" films, and the elite Irving Theater, which ran all of the latest and greatest hits. Films were offered daily—afternoons and evenings. Although people did not dine out as frequently as now, the city had a number of excellent restaurants, including a number of specialty restaurants offering Italian cuisine and the new food craze, pizza. For sweet treats, there were a number of ice cream parlors as well as restaurants that specialized in particular desserts.

Although the city had once maintained a semi-professional baseball club, by the 1950s this had ceased to exist, but there were numerous small neighborhood or club-associated baseball teams located in various sections of the town. The city was very sports-focused and supported the various high school teams, mainly in baseball and basketball, and, to a lesser degree, in football. In order to encourage sports and exercise, as well as for general entertainment in summer months, the city maintained a number of playgrounds, organized by community leaders in local neighborhoods and partly supported by these, but organized around a Playground Association, led by administrators and teachers employed by the Carbondale School District. For this, the school board allotted a budget that provided various materials, hired Carbondale college students to work with the youth at respective playgrounds, supported several larger all-playground events, such as the annual "Kiddies Day" held at Newton Lake, a series of sports competitions among the playgrounds, and an evening all-playgounds Dance Review at Russell Park. Individual playground associations raised additional monies to provide daily activities and special events for the children, purchase playground equipment, prepare playing fields, and build field houses.[16]

All in all, Carbondale was a nice little American city in the years of the late 1940s and early 1950s. Carbondale of this era was a place that, in spite of some clear evidence of economic decline, residents and former residents today look back on with no small amount of nostalgia, and keen memories of past events, places, and people. But no one remembers anyone foretelling the horrendous fate soon to befall this pleasant community, caused by the insidious fire below its surface.

Chapter 3:

The Underground Inferno

"We were about as far down as a town could go," a Carbondale resident told *The Kiwanis Magazine* in June 1965.[1] The 1950s and '60s had become a cascade of catastrophe for Carbondale. As the mines closed and the railroads shut down, unemployment soared, and the population was in startlingly rapid decline. The Kiwanis article's focus was the "fantastically stubborn and cunning" fire, which in the view of its author was potentially a saving grace for the city. His take on the situation was that the huge and costly efforts being taken to extinguish the fire and rebuild the affected neighborhood were likely to be a boon to the declining city. But most Carbondalians, especially those who lived directly on top of the mine fire, did not share his optimism.

How did this nightmare begin? Most people who lived through it and most mine fire experts say that the fire began as a result of the city's dumping refuse into abandoned strip-mine pits on the northwestern edge of the West Side. These pits, which had been the Hudson Coal Company's Powderly Mine, were located along Fallbrook Creek, a small stream running southward from Fell Township to Brooklyn Street in Carbondale, where the creek emptied into the Lackawanna River. No one lived in the dumping area itself, but several streets with homes on them were located nearby. The abandoned strip mines near the dump contained outcroppings of coal partially hidden in the earth and rock. The official summary of the fire prepared by the United States Bureau of Mines reports that these pits were used as a garbage dump by the city of Carbondale for about five years, during which time the mine fire was ignited.[2]

Whether this dump was set afire by an act of nature or man is not known, but the trash fire ignited the coal. The fire then bled into underground coal deposits, igniting discarded carbonaceous material and the exposed surface of coal beds along the high walls of the pits.[3] An article appearing in *Time* Magazine in August 1956 puts the date of onset of the mine fire at 1943.[4] It was evident that a mine fire existed in this area at least as early as 1943. Residents of the West Side had begun noticing hot areas along the creek bank, and recalled that the ground in this area was never covered by snow or ice in the winter. Steam and sulfur-laced vapor were observed coming from the ground.[5]

According to an article in *The Saturday Evening Post* in 1963,[6] in the beginning, West Side residents regarded this as "more a nuisance than a menace." The West Siders who were interviewed for this study agree. Though no one could say with any certitude when the fire had begun, everyone agreed that they accepted the fire's reality early on. Most people initially believed that the fire would not spread to their area of the West Side or that it would harm them.

According to residents' recollections, the only people who really were bothered by, or even noticed the signs of fire, were those living in the North Scott Street area near Fallbrook Creek.[7] Helen and Catherine Kane, who lived further south on Scott Street, remembered walking their dog on the creek's banks and the hot ground hurting the animal's paws.[8] Several other residents talked about witnessing steam escaping from the ground in this area in the late 1940s.[9]

The city of Carbondale began a modest mine fire control project in the late 1940s and early 1950s which involved flushing the fire by pouring large quantities of water into the burning areas and making small excavations in various locations nearby. This was a conventional approach to attacking mine fires at the time. The technique involved using fire hoses to pour large quantities of water into the pit. Then a layer of wet clay was rolled across the area to seal off oxygen and suffocate the flames. The U.S. Bureau of Mines assisted in this effort, which was said to have cost $200,000 before it was discontinued; it also involved dumping more than 80,000 cubic yards of noncombustible silt.[10]

This first attempt was the proverbial pouring money down a hole. During this early period of the fire, when it appeared to be concentrated near the dump, city fathers believed the fire could be extinguished by flushing. But the fire continued to spread, fed by air from both subterranean and surface sources. As this reality was gradually recognized in the early to mid 1950s, the next step involved the use of boreholes of up to one hundred feet that were drilled around areas believed to be the fire's perimeter. Sand, silt, and other materials were flushed down to build barriers to wall in the fire. When Thomas Gilmartin, then editor of *The Carbondale Daily News* and a resident of the West Side, was interviewed in 1965, he said, "For a time, that seemed to work. The fire seemed to burn itself out, and we all had peace of mind."[11] Ultimately, however, these measures were viewed as unsuccessful and were discontinued for lack of funds. Remarked one retired miner, "It was a business of too little and too late."[12]

Up to this point, say former residents of Carbondale's West Side, they continued to live their lives pretty much as usual. Many, particularly those who lived near the dumping pits and the creek bed, harbored some concern about the spreading mine fire. But those in other areas of the West Side and Carbondalians in general, inspired by the thinking that the fire seemed concentrated in a relatively small area of the West Side, clung to the hope that it would burn itself out or that the flushing effort would snuff it out.

People were aware that a mine fire was burning beneath a section of the West Side, but were not particularly bothered by it. They believed that it was limited to a small uninhabited area. The West Side of Carbondale was a working-class region for the most part, and the people who lived there thought of themselves as tough, no-nonsense individuals who were used to handling situations that came their way. This was just another problem with which they would cope. The rest of the city of Carbondale seemed safely distant from the concerns of a small segment of the West Side and its mine fire.

The Danger Comes to the Surface

That was the attitude until November 14, 1952. Everything changed the day Patrick and Elizabeth Collins, an elderly couple who lived some distance from Fallbrook Creek on North Scott Street, were discovered dead. Later, when *The Saturday Evening Post* interviewed West Sider Jim Collins, a nephew of the Collins couple, he recalled that morning: "One day we noticed through the window that the table at my uncle's house next door was set but we didn't see him or my aunt. The next day the table was still set exactly the same way. We got worried. The door was locked, so we broke in."[13] Inside they found Mr. and Mrs. Collins, dead.[14]

Due to the sudden nature of their deaths, medical examinations of their bodies were called for. This confirmed that the deaths were due to carbon monoxide—carbon monoxide that came from the mine fire. The mine fire had killed! Somehow, this deadly gas had gotten into the Collins home and had silently taken their lives.

Given the location of the Collins home, this meant that the fire had now spread several blocks from the original site. According to Dr. Thomas Coleman, the couple's physician who participated in the autopsy, their deaths changed everything about the mine fire.[15] Now the earlier view that the fire was essentially an annoyance was replaced by the reality that a deadly menace existed in Carbondale—a menace that threatened more than property and that could not be ignored or wished away. And there was more to come.

Soon after the tragic deaths of Patrick and Elizabeth Collins, high concentrations of the gas were discovered in several homes along Scott Street and east to South Hospital Street—an area that had not previously been involved with the fire. On a Sunday morning a short time later, some fifty people were nearly overcome by carbon monoxide gas in their homes and would have certainly died but for the lucky circumstance that they were up and about, preparing for Mass.[16] Several people became dizzy and nauseated; in a neighborhood full of miners and retired miners, many quickly recognized the symptoms and hurried outside their houses. People called to their neighbors, and what could have been a mass tragedy was averted. A number were examined by doctors who confirmed that carbon monoxide had indeed been the cause of their illness.[17] Fear now replaced complacency. Carbondale Mayor Frank Kelly, interviewed by *The Saturday Evening Post,* said that changing air currents in the mine made it possible for carbon monoxide to creep into West Side homes.[18] All Carbondale—and especially all West Side residents—now knew no one was safe.

Memories abound of the Collins tragedy and the nearly deadly experiences that West Siders now began to have as the fire continued to spread to eventually encompass more than 80 percent of the West Side. Edward Spall, a youngster at the time, recalled years later that his family, who lived on Willow Avenue, off Brooklyn Street on the extreme southwestern edge of the West Side—and thus some distance from the original site—had to move out of their house one Christmas Eve due to high concentrations of carbon monoxide.[19] Mr. Spall recalled that he believes he first heard about the mine fire when Mr. and Mrs. Collins died, and that at that time there was some worry about whether or not it might affect them, but that the adults in his family "kept their concerns to themselves so as not to concern us."[20]

"65 Willow Avenue in Carbondale – The Spall Home" – Courtesy of Edward Spall

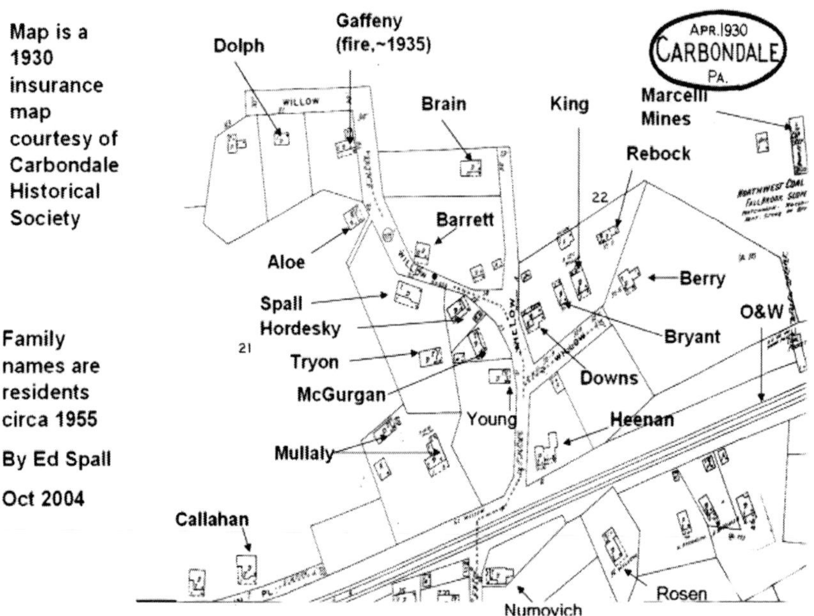

"Gobblers Knob Map – A Section of the West Side Affected by the Mine Fire" – Courtesy of Edward Spall

This view was echoed by many of those interviewed for this study. Mary Louise Germano Nepa, another former resident of Carbondale's West Side, recalls that as a child, she first heard about the mine fire from her parents. Mrs. Nepa lived in relatively close proximity to the original site of the fire, on Scott Street, and says that her family was scared that the fire might harm them. She also recalls that her family felt helpless in the face of the situation: "Relatives and friends were worried for our health and safety" and "wanted us to move away."[21] She also recalls that there were suspicions that some untimely deaths of neighbors were related to carbon monoxide poisoning.[22]

The connection between the carbon monoxide deaths of the Collinses and other unexpected or sudden deaths of West Side residents remains a vivid memory for many of those interviewed for this study. Although none but the Collins couple were officially listed as having died as a result of carbon monoxide poisoning, suspicions remain that other West Siders who died suddenly in this time period were actually victims of the mine fire.

Following the Collins tragedy, Carbondale officials, led by Mayor Frank Kelly and officials of the Hudson Coal Company that owned most of the coal in the mine fire region, now recognized the danger it posed to both life and property. It was also apparent that the fire had spread and had the potential to spread over a much larger area, including north and south of the city to neighboring towns, since virtually all of Carbondale and the surrounding region was underlain with both unmined coal and abandoned mines.

The enormity of the problem and the financial costs that would be involved in eradicating it spurred city and mining officials to request federal assistance. Federal mining experts from the U.S. Bureau of Mines were sent to the region to investigate. They subsequently submitted a number of reports attesting to the seriousness of the situation, and the risks to the life, health, and property of persons living on Carbondale's West Side. These reports also confirmed the spread of the fire. The U.S. Bureau of Mines made recommendations for measures to control the fire and gave estimates of the costs involved.[23]

The mine investigators concluded that the carbon monoxide from the burning coal had risen into the Collins house through cracks in the basement. The incident on Scott Street proved that the poisonous gas was a deadly hazard to people even if where they lived showed no surface signs of the fire. In a neighborhood where the vast majority of the men were coal miners or retired coal miners, carbon monoxide was a familiar foe. Most of them had already decided that that was what had killed Mr. and Mrs. Collins, and they were already sure that many other illnesses sprang from the same cause.[24]

The fire's spread was due to its eating its way from the dump site into abandoned mines that honeycombed the earth below the West Side. Some of the veins of coal in these mines had been mined years earlier; coal remained loose and scattered about in the chambers. The leftover coal and gasses that were trapped in the chambers and the coal pillars that had supported the workings of the mines fed the fire. This was not an unusual occurrence in mining regions. One article reported that in 1965 the U.S. Department of Mines listed some 220 underground active mine fires in the United States; more than seventy alone were located in the bituminous coal fields of western Pennsylvania.[25]

The immediate situation facing Carbondale was dire, and Mayor Kelly acted swiftly and decisively. Mayor Kelly, described in *The Saturday Evening Post* article as "a soft-spoken, grandfatherly-looking man," was Carbondale's chief administrator from 1952 through 1960—during what he called "the town's worst years of crisis."[26] Despite the opposition of some people who thought the problem should be dealt with locally, Kelly declared a state of emergency and requested assistance from both the federal and state governments' bureaus of mines. Soon, federal and state mining inspectors joined Carbondale policemen in disaster-prevention efforts. By the mid 1950s, mine inspectors armed with gas detectors conducted 24-hour surveys of homes in the mine fire area, checking for carbon monoxide (CO) and carbon dioxide (CO_2).

Guardian Angels with Gas Detectors

Inspector Martin Campbell described one particular situation he encountered. He located "gas in one cellar and went upstairs to warn the lone resident. . . . I found her in the kitchen knocked out. . . . I got her outside and called the police and told them to send a doctor. Fifteen minutes more . . . and she would have been dead."[27] Mine inspectors like Mr. Campbell became a common sight in the affected area as they went about their daily checks for dangerous gases. Resident Andy Cerra said in a 1995 interview which appeared in the regional newspaper, *The Sunday Times*, "Twice a day the guy would come with his machine and check your cellar for carbon monoxide. He was like one of the family after awhile."[28] Mary Louise Germano Nepa recalls, "We had a gauge (for gas readings) in our house to check on the carbon monoxide levels all the time. If there were signs of coal gas we were evacuated fast."[29] She does not recall having to leave her home because of the gas, but many others who were interviewed do remember.

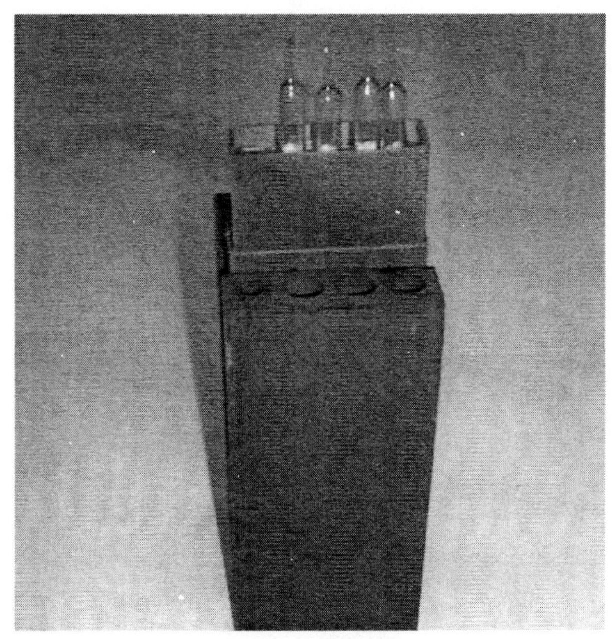

"Gas Testing Equipment 1" –
Courtesy of Rosemary Grizzanti

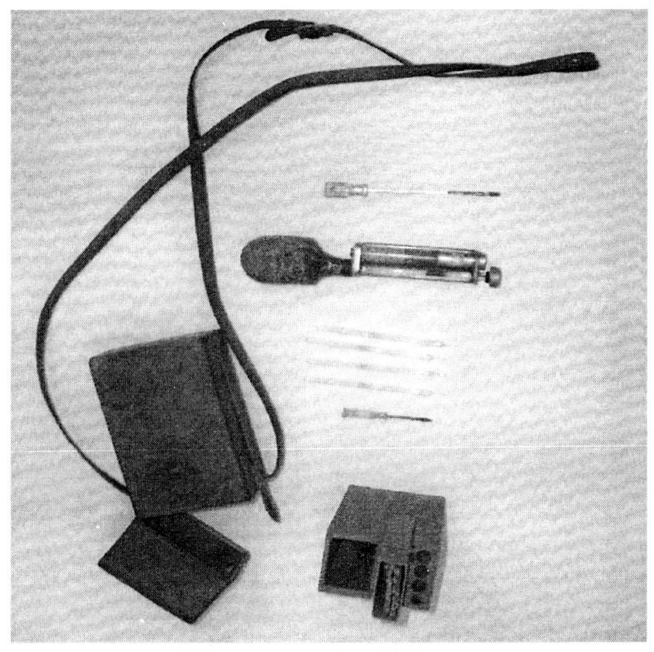

"Gas Testing Equipment 2" –
Courtesy of Rosemary Grizzanti

"Gas Testing Equipment 3" –
Courtesy of Rosemary Grizzanti

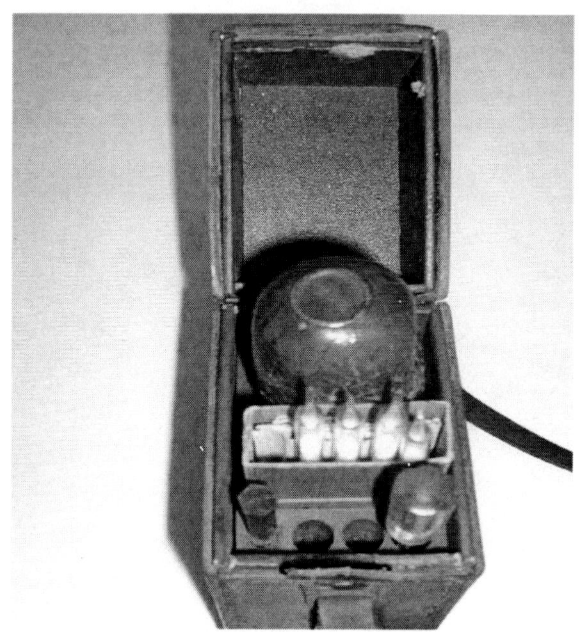

"Gas Testing Equipment 4" –
Courtesy of Rosemary Grizzanti

As the fire spread, the flushing efforts intensified. Edward Spall recalls the impact this process had on his family's life. "Approximately eight to ten holes were drilled on our property in an attempt to extinguish the fire. The constant banging of the impact drills they used, the mess made of our lawn and the street from the trucks carrying silt, and the fire hoses used to flush the stuff down the holes—it was quite a disaster as far as destroying the peacefulness and good looks of the neighborhood. Also, the [mine] inspectors would come into your home three times a day, once at about 3:00 AM. Many times I awoke to see the inspector sampling the air over my head in bed. We got used to it."[30] Many of the people interviewed for this work described the same kind of relationship developing between their families and the inspectors. The inspectors became "family" because they were the first line of defense against the menace of the deadly gas.

Rosemary Tryon Grizzanti remembers that the mine inspectors came three times a day and at night. Families kept their doors open for the inspectors to get in. The inspectors went around the homes with a tester, checking corners of rooms near the ceilings for gas. Mrs. Grizzanti's family was forced to leave their home twice—once on Christmas day, when they went to her aunt's home and stayed there until the gas cleared out. She remembers being given oxygen at least once, which may have been due to her breathing in some gas. She recounted the friendship that developed between her family and the inspectors and had a picture taken with one inspector that indicates the closeness they felt for him.[31]

Other interviewees tell similar stories. West Siders came to place great trust in the inspectors. They left their front doors and cellars unlocked around the clock, so the inspectors had constant access to their houses. So strong was the fear of the gas that people "set their alarm clocks, got up once an hour through the night, and roused sleepers to make sure that all were safe."[32] Many people who were interviewed for this study say that their parents—particularly their fathers or other males in the family, many of whom were coal miners or former coal miners who were acutely aware of the dangers involved with gas—slept very little at night. Seeing the mine inspectors coming into the homes and making their checks for gas was the only thing that assured homeowners and their families that it was safe to continue to live in their homes. They and the inspectors often forged a solid relationship built on the realities of this most stressful situation.

Mine inspectors were now reporting frequent "showings" of the light odorless deadly carbon monoxide in upper stories of West Side homes. In addition, gas checks were showing evidence of the heavier carbon dioxide—CO_2 or "black damp"—located mainly in cellars and sometimes in large concentrations. "If you walked into it," said one mine inspector, "you'd last only as long as the air in your lungs lasted."[33] Mrs. Grizzanti attested to this by telling about her pet chickens that were taken into the cellar in the colder months. They were overcome by this gas, and several died as a result.[34]

Fearful residents of the mine fire area, now designated by Pennsylvania State Mine inspectors as the "mine fire zone," slept with their windows open no matter how cold or wet the weather. Neighbors watched over each other. Dr. Coleman, who had many West Siders among his patients, recalled the physical hardships the people of this area were forced to endure as the mine fire situation worsened. He treated many for respiratory illnesses triggered by the cold (and probably also by the stress).[35]

Although West Siders worked frantically to seal up cracks in their homes, the fire relentlessly continued to propel the gas, which entered homes through the cracks or by following water pipes. Inspector teams were forced on many occasions to order people from their homes, or inspectors had to return for hourly checks on the concentration of gas in homes in the event that it would become necessary to alert people of the need to evacuate the home. "We lived in fear," said retired coal miner William Cooper, a lifelong West Sider.[36]

It was especially bad in winter, not only because of the need to leave windows open but also because outdoor outlets for the fire's exhaust froze over and changes in air currents in the mines caused the gases to surge into homes. "Black damp" carbon dioxide extinguished furnace fires on many subzero nights, so residents woke to cold houses and frozen pipes.

Local hotels were used to house people who had no family or friends to turn to for shelter if they were forced to leave their homes. Evacuation could turn into an expensive proposition, because sometimes families were removed for several days and even weeks before gas concentration levels fell low enough for them to return to their homes. In these events, the Red Cross helped pay for the lodging.[37]At the time, Mayor Kelly lamented, "Entire families aren't living—they're existing."[38]

"Brooklyn Street Looking South in the Area Now McDonalds" – Courtesy of William J. Connor

"LOOKING TOWARD SCRANTON ON A RAINY DAY" –
COURTESY OF WILLIAM J. CONNOR

More Signs of the Fire

On top of the constant fear of poison gas and daily confrontations with mounting inconveniences from the flushing operations, increasing evidence of the fire began to appear on the surface. Cracks and sinking spots on the ground triggered worries for the West Siders about what was going to happen to them and their homes in the long run. And more importantly, how were they, mostly retired miners and working-class people, going to be able to afford the costs of repair and recovery?

Virtually no one envisioned government assistance for them beyond what the city was already doing to try to put out the fire. West Siders experienced many sleepless nights worrying about the future, and according to comments made by interviewees, parents kept their concerns to themselves so as not to worry their children—a circumstance much like the reported "whispered worry" found in similar circumstances during the Great Depression.

Things kept getting worse. Heated ground on the West side, evidence of the fire's spread upward toward the earth's surface, wreaked havoc. Not only did it melt snow and keep grass green even in the winter months, but it also heated concrete foundations to a point where residents could hardly walk into their basements. With the heat came vapor rising from floors and walls. Occasionally, as if a vicious evil mind with cruel intent was at work below ground, the fire would emit bursts of sound—subsurface gas explosions—frightening residents all the more.

In the mid-1950s, even children who had been shielded from knowing much, if anything, about the fire were becoming more aware of the disastrous situation. One child, who lived on badly affected Scott Street, told a *Pageant Magazine* reporter, "Thank God we're alive."[39] Many of the people interviewed for this book were children at the time of the fire. The facts and details they recall about this period are testimony to the remarkable degree of understanding they had of what was happening. Their memories of the fire are clear and reveal a deep understanding of particulars about the fire and its effects on their parents and neighbors. Some of this is due, no doubt, to the fact that when the fire first became apparent many of them were in elementary school, but in its later stages, they were teenagers and young adults. In a real sense, these people grew up with the mine fire in their lives.

Meanwhile, some newspapers took a more lighthearted approach to Carbondale's mine fire, and one nicknamed the West Side "Monoxide Gardens."[40] But few Carbondalians, then or now, saw the fire as funny. Former residents interviewed for this study were asked if they recalled any humorous situations involving this period. Everyone stated that they recalled nothing that could be called comical about this time.

An unidentified doctor who said he treated West Siders, remarked that it was "hard to comprehend" what living on the West Side had become for its residents. He asked, "How can a person have peace of mind enough to sleep when he knows, 'Well, I'll go to sleep now, but maybe I won't wake up?' Or when he works the late shift and leaves the house at midnight, not knowing what he may find when he comes home?"[41]

It was tension and terror all the time. But the worse was still to come.

Chapter 4:

The Big Dig-Out Project

By the mid 1950s, investigations of the Carbondale mine fire had determined that it had spread under the West Side to directly affect a surface area of about 120 acres, and was burning down to a depth of about one hundred feet. According to mining records, the first forty feet below surface were wash and rock, and below that there were five to six coal veins of varying degrees of density, ranging from three to eight feet and separated by layers of slate and sand. Mining experts suspected that in the mined and unmined labyrinth, the fire might be feeding at one level under one area and at a lower or higher level on the next. Surges of CO and CO_2 were not accurate indications of the fire's location. About the only way to estimate where the fire really was burning was to take comparative temperature readings at the various boreholes. Sometimes these readings reached highs of 750 to 900 degrees Fahrenheit on thermometers that melted before they were raised.[1]

As the fire spread under more of the West Side, heat and cave-ins added to the people's plight. Cave-ins, a constant in mining areas, became a fact of life for West Siders. Leo Coleman, a railroader who lived in the mine fire area, described one incident he suffered: "Just after [I] had ordered two tons of coal and had it delivered to [my] cellar, a big cave-in came right under the coal and the whole pile went down in the mines. It took everything."[2] The fire, according to Mr. Coleman, was so close and so real that the ground under the home "quivered and sank. . . . We couldn't take anyone into the parlor. . . . The wallpaper there was torn, everything was busted and there was plaster falling all over everything. They jacked up the house four times, but it would sink again."[3]

"Cellars," said a *The Saturday Evening Post* magazine reporter, "became forests of jacks as householders struggled to keep their homes upright."[4] Such efforts were not always successful. Stanley Cominsky reported that his home "continued to tilt until it was hard to walk across the floors without slipping."[5] Cominsky "propped the teetering structure with boards, but it still threatened to tip over."[6] Mr. Cominsky went on, "The walls were busted, the sewer and water pipes leaking, and everything was falling apart."[7] Many residents faced situations like Mr. Cominsky's, but they had very few, if any, options. They could move, but who would purchase a home that was literally falling apart? Most residents could not afford to just move on and abandon a wrecked house.

Even more than their financial investments, West Siders were rooted in their neighborhoods by deep emotional ties. They loved their houses, many of which had been built by their parents or grandparents. Each home was part of a family's "American Dream." To West Siders, their properties were truly irreplaceable. Every West Side landowner had lawns and gardens, which they tended with loving care and in which they took great pride. In addition to flowers and shrubs, many properties boasted large vegetable gardens and fruit-bearing trees. During the Great Depression, when so many people were out of work, it was the pride of the West Side that no one went hungry because everyone grew food and shared it with neighbors.

A close community, the West Side consisted of several distinct neighborhoods where people knew not only each other, but each other's parents, grandparents, and extended families. West Siders' lives, as well as their fortunes, were deeply interwoven with ties that bound them to their properties, to their neighbors, and to their community. Moving on was not an option. They had to stay and pray that somehow the situation could be rectified.

As time went on, inspectors reported that the fire was so close to the surface that the soles of their feet were burned as they checked cellars. The smell of burning sulfur became a constant. Interviewees recall the foul smell of "burning eggs" coming from the boreholes.[8] The ground on the play area at one of the West Side schools was too hot to stand on—even during snowy, frigid winter months.

Losing Hope and Homes

As their neat and proudly maintained homes and gardens started showing the effects of the ravaging fire, many West Siders began to give up. Windows broke, paint blistered, porches were tilted by mine cave-ins—"caves." Every day a new crack or mine subsidence testified to the terrible situation. Resident John Gilroy lamented to a reporter, "After all those years . . . we got the garden fixed, we transplanted the roses to where they'd grow just right. We even had a fish pool, and, I tell you, the place was one of the sights of the West Side when we had it right. It's hard to see it going by degrees."[9]

Cave-ins caused some of the streets to rise or drop and crack. Houses tilted and swayed. Efforts of the city to repair street subsidences proved fruitless. Sinkholes dotted the streets; sewers ruptured and had to be repaired. Patching seemed a waste of time and money since the patches broke up almost immediately.

"Even nature," said Henry Lee, writing in *Pageant* magazine, "looks tired along the West Side. Dead trees, stripped of their bark, and dying shrubs abound in the neighborhood. Because of the heat . . . grass grows even in the winter, but year-round it is a dull, faded green."[10] The entire landscape had the look of the surreal with smoke emitting from the ground and strange rumblings echoing from below. Each day was a challenge and each day could bring disaster.

Five-year-old Bob Perri, who lived on Ontario Street, walked across the lawn of his family's home on a summer day in 1955 with a pitcher of lemonade his mother had made, and he was nearly swallowed up when the ground behind him caved in. Referring to Bob Perri's father, Santo Perri, *The Saturday Evening Post* reported this:

> As he took the pitcher from the child, Bob screamed, 'Daddy, the ground is falling.'" Mr. Perri said he "looked down and didn't know what to think. The ground was opening underneath

him. I grabbed him by the shoulder and threw him behind me. Everything went down and it kept going down and down. I flung myself back away from the hole and clawed up the bank. Mr. Perri continued, "When it went down, this debris and thick yellow smoke and flame came up out of the hole. Some men up on Willow Avenue about a half mile away saw it and thought the house was on fire."

Perri, Son Almost Engulfed As Earth Caves, Spews Fire

Santo Perri, 51 Ontario St., and his young son, Bobby, had a narrow escape from death this afternoon about 1:15 as the ground caved almost under their feet and spewed flame, smoke and fumes to the height of a house roof.

The two were walking in the yard at the rear of the Perri home when Bobby looked behind him.

"Look, Daddy," he cried.

When his father turned he saw the earth caving behind them. The two ran to safety and crew working on a flushing project immediately adjacent to the cave scrambled back also.

Eyewitnesses told the NEWS that blue flame, yellow, black and white smoke roared into the air. When a NEWS reporter and photographer arrived at the scene about 20 minutes later white smoke and vapor were visible, but not the more colorful manifestations.

However, waves of heat could be seen dancing above the cave, which was about 10 feet across.

A crowd from the neighborhood gathered quickly as word of the incident spread.

The performance was by far the most spectacular staged by the mine fire to date, although it is blamed for two deaths due to carbon monoxide.

The fire, which is described as having started in a city dumping ground in a stripping west of Scott St. in 1946, now has spread over a great area. There is evidence of fire from N. Scott St. south to Poplar St. To the west the fire has spread to the top of Willow Ave. and to the east hot boreholes have been drilled on Devine Ave.

An elaborate drilling and flushing program proposed by the Pennsylvania Department of Mines is stalemated at present for a lack of waivers permitting access to properties involved. There now is evidence of active fire east of the perimeter drawn up in the state's plan.

Meanwhile a limited federal project is being completed. The flushing which was being done on the Perri property when the cave occurred is a part of this U. S. program.

CARBONDALE SUBSIDENCE—Pictured above is large cave hole which occurred in Carbondale's West Side mine fire area yesterday afternoon and in which a Carbondale man and his six-year-old son narrowly escaped being engulfed. The settlement is approximately 15 to 20 feet in diameter and of unknown depth. Some steam is evident escaping from the fissure in the above photo. (Tribune Photo by Bill Nally)

VIEW INTO CAVE which almost engulfed Santo Perri and his son Bobby yesterday afternoon is shown above left. Manifestations of mine fire which were so spectacular when cave first occurred had simmered down considerably this morning when NEWS cameraman poked his head, and his camera, over the edge of the void to take this picture. Waves of heat still blasted him, however, and left no question as to whether the fire was alive. Some fill had been dumped into the void before picture was snapped, but there remained plenty of filling to be done. Darkest patch in photo at center bottom is old mine working, which points in the direction of Brooklyn St. Hundreds of people visited the scene yesterday afternoon and last night, and again this morning sightseers were making their way there. Picture above right shows some of the neighborhood residents who gathered in the rain yesterday afternoon directly after cave occurred and fire and smoke spilled out of ground. (Mickev Schella photos).

"Perri and Son Near Tragedy" –
Courtesy of Angelo Mazza et al.

Mr. Perri, described in the *Post* article as a "short, dark, powerfully built ex-railroader, father of eight," who almost perished in trying to rescue his son, exclaimed, "Mother of God, we could have been cooked alive."[11]

Despite earlier efforts of Carbondale and the Pennsylvania Department of Mines, mine experts in the 1960s finally acknowledged what West Side residents already knew—the mine fire was still spreading. According to mining records, three anthracite mining beds were now involved.[12] The U.S. Bureau of Mines techniques for fighting mine fires—flushing, drilling boreholes, and pouring silt down on mine fields—had shown little success (at great cost) elsewhere, and they were equally futile in Carbondale.[13]

Faced with nearly a decade of failure to even contain, let alone extinguish, the fire, city and mining experts from the state of Pennsylvania turned to experimental methods, such as "bleeders"—small boreholes on residents' property. Someone suggested digging large shafts to ventilate the chambers and draw off the fumes. But mining experts pointed out that more likely this would just feed oxygen and fire it up further. At this point, ideas—many of which were creative but impractical—came in from all over the world. One "engineer" wrote that "for $100,000, Carbondale could drain off its nearby lakes into the mine and flood the fire."[14] Someone offered the idea that the mine pits should be stuffed with dry ice to kill the flames, but given the spread of the fire, this idea lacked merit. One European "expert" offered to come to Carbondale and eradicate the fire—if his transportation were provided—but he refused to divulge a plan.[15]

Money was a major problem. At this time, the Federal Bureau of Mines had never allocated more than $200,000 a year to fight mine fires in the United States, and only a part of this had been earmarked for Carbondale. Many people involved with fighting the fire believed that the state government should be putting up more of the costs. The city itself was in danger of exhausting all of its dwindling resources dealing with the fire.

Carbondale and most of northeastern Pennsylvania did not really share in the economic good times the rest of the country experienced in the 1950s and early '60s. Though some other industries survived the demise of anthracite mining, the region's economy had been almost completely based on mining. Unemployment increased steadily through the decade of the '50s, which caused the population to shrink as many younger workers and their families moved out. The situation was already bleak before the fire. Now, however, the sliding economy of Carbondale as well as earlier expenditures to contain the fire meant that the city had very limited funds to contribute to any new effort to eliminate the fire. Shrinking its taxable base further was the fact that the city had begun to cut property taxes on some West Side properties afflicted by the terrible conditions caused by the fire. Faced with a failed effort and no further available funds, drilling and flushing was discontinued—at least until more funds became available. But, as *The Carbondale Daily News* editor Tom Gilmartin said, "The fire was . . . twenty-four hours a day, every day. It didn't operate on a fiscal year."[16]

Blight from Below

Experts now began to state the obvious: the only way to destroy this menace was to dig it out. But to do so would require removal of an entire section of the city of Carbondale and the people who lived there. Further, this would necessitate the purchase of properties located in the fire zone. Once these properties were purchased, buildings would be razed and the area stripped to remove every ounce of coal down to the bedrock. In all, about 120 acres inhabited by thirteen hundred people would be stripped.[17]

Faced with the reality of the situation, Carbondale turned the project over to the Carbondale Redevelopment Authority, an entity already in place created to foster redevelopment projects throughout the city. Mining experts from the Federal Bureau of Mines said that the fire could be conquered by digging it out, but, aware of Carbondale's precarious finances, they questioned the source of funding for such an enormous undertaking. The Hudson Coal Company, one of the largest coal companies in the area, owned mineral rights to the entire area, but surface rights to only a few acres. West Side residents occupied an area representing between four hundred and five hundred properties that were privately owned. Neither the Hudson Coal Company nor the city of Carbondale could afford this buyout.

In January 1956, Mayor Kelly and a number of prominent Carbondalians, including C. B. Tomaine, a well-known civic leader and local businessman, attended a two-day conference in nearby Scranton. There, they heard a description of the newly created Federal Urban Renewal Program. One of the speakers told of government grants under the program available to cities to remove "areas of blight." Mayor Kelly recalled, "He was talking about slum clearance . . . but we suddenly realized that blight can occur below ground as well as above."[18]

At first the U.S. government was dubious about the idea of below-ground blight. But Carbondale civic leaders, including the Greater Carbondale Chamber of Commerce, the Carbondale-Lackawanna Development Company, and others, began to lobby for the project. Republican Congressman Joseph L. Carrigg of the 10th Congressional District (who two years earlier had told a Carbondale Citizens Committee that prayer would be more effective than petitions in getting help from the federal government)[19] jumped onboard in a show of bipartisan support for the "big dig," proving, as the *The Carbondale Daily News* stated that "carbon monoxide molecules have equal affinity for Democratic and Republican red blood corpuscles."[20]

The Federal Housing and Home Financing Agency became interested in the idea that underground blight would render a community eligible for urban redevelopment grants. Regional Administrator David Walker noted, "Nowhere else have we had the problem of digging out a fire, extinguishing it and then backfilling and reusing the land."[21] Scranton Redevelopment Authority Administrator Bernard Blier said that the Carbondale project was a first, and became a model for other similar projects in the nation.[22] In the end, Carbondale received approval for its mine fire project some four months after submitting the proposal—said to be a record time, one-third as long as was usually required for approval of federal grants.[23]

The Mine Fire Project became a reality—or, as some remember it, a nightmare.

It entailed digging huge V-shape ditches, sixty to one-hundred-ten feet deep and three times as wide, on the outer perimeters of the West Side, to constitute a buttress region. Then, very deliberately, massive dragline shovels dug down and inward, and dragged out all the coal and stone, burning or not. It was trucked it away, and the land was backfilled and graded.

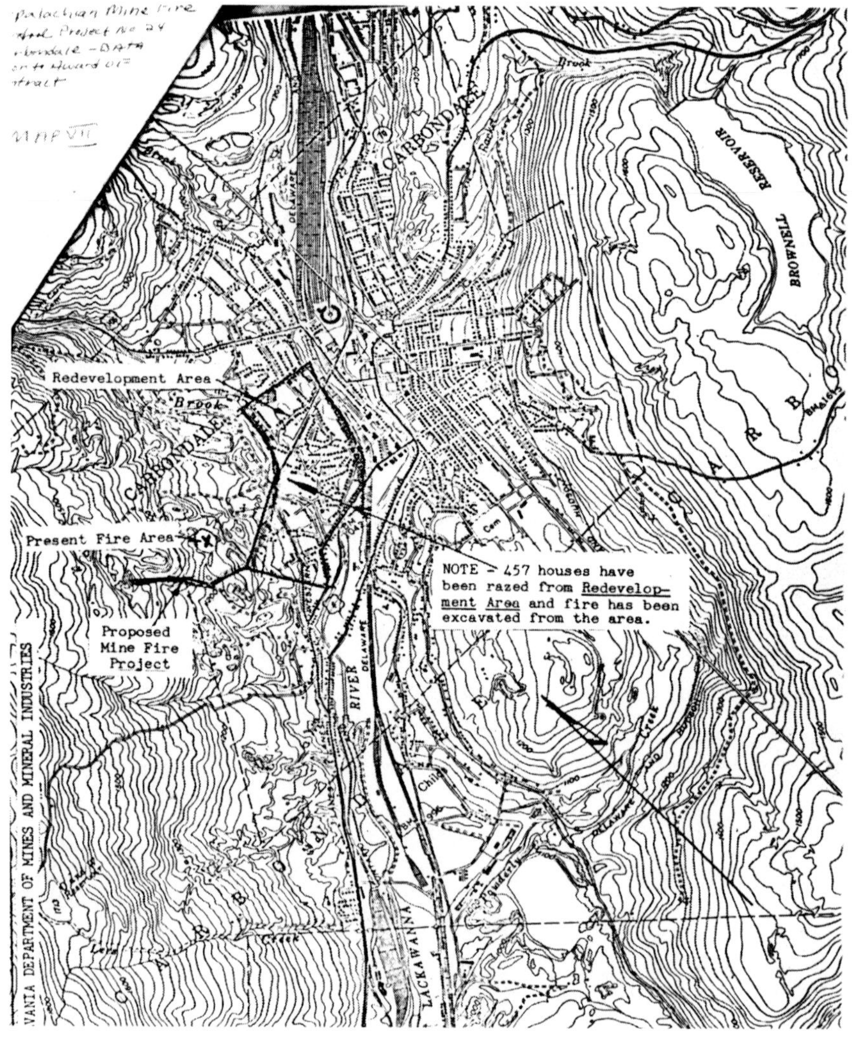

"AERIAL VIEW OF MINE FIRE REGION" – COURTESY OF THE FEDERAL DEPARTMENT OF MINES

Rehabilitation of a Former Mine Fire Area

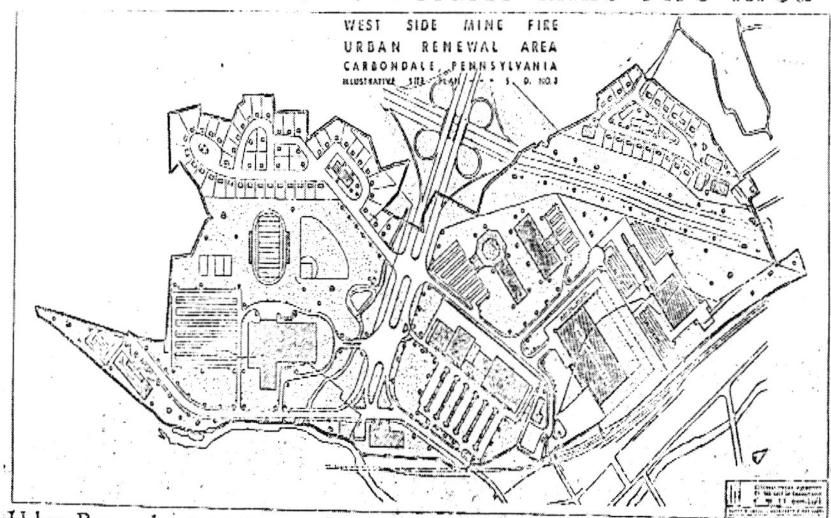

Urban Renewal Takes Over

It took 25 years to conquer Carbondale's massive underground blaze and to reach the point at which restoration of the surface showed concrete results.

...reation, commercial and industrial projects which is evolving through the efforts of the Carbondale Redevelopment Authority in Lackawanna County.

"REHABILITATION PLAN FOR MINE FIRE REGION" –
COURTESY OF THE FEDERAL DEPARTMENT OF MINES

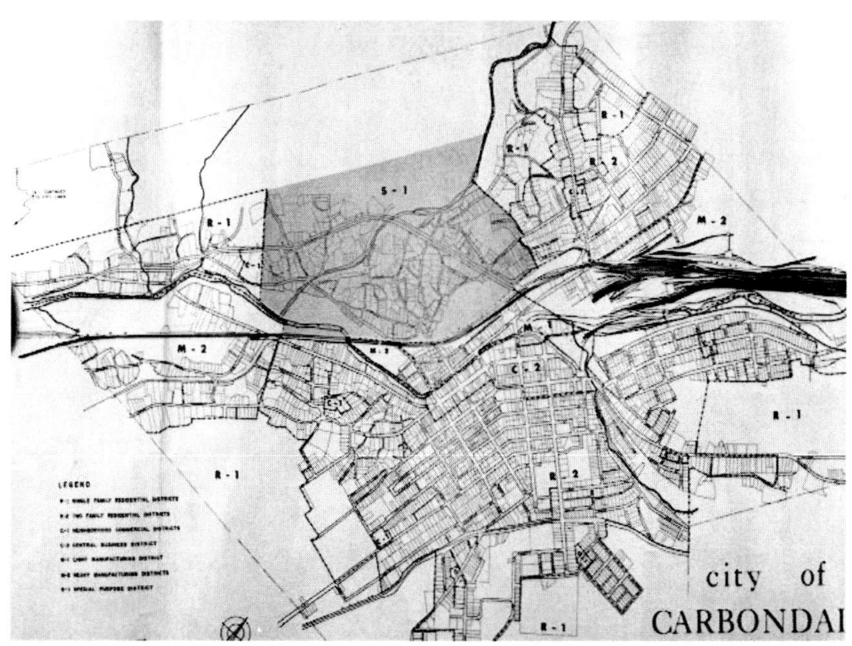

"VIEW OF MINE FIRE PROJECT AREA" –
COURTESY OF THE FEDERAL DEPARTMENT OF MINES

"A nasty job," said mining engineer Robert W. Bell, consultant to the Carbondale Redevelopment Authority, ". . . rather dangerous . . . the dragline operators will be only the length of their booms (sixty to ninety feet) away from the hot stuff. Each scoopful will be dumped on high ground and sprayed with water," he went on. "In many places the hot surface will have to be covered with clay to keep truck tires from softening."[24]

One estimate put the cost of the project at about $2 million. Two-thirds was federal money for acquisition of the land. Pennsylvania was said to have put up $1 million. The remainder came from Carbondale with money secured by the city from royalties on coal recovered during the digging and the resale of the stripped land.[25] Another estimate put these figures slightly higher: $2.8 million from the federal government for land acquisition; $1.1 million from the state.[26]

Although the West Side mine fire had been burning below-surface coal for years, mining engineers estimated that there were still more than 2.2 million tons of usable coal below in the ground.[27] This coal could be dug out by steam shovels and hauled away. This plan had already been on the drawing boards of the Carbondale Coal Company prior to the mine fire emergency and that company was already conducting strip-mining operations on Carbondale's West Side. But the company could not strip-mine all of the coal because of private property on the land. Now, however, that impediment was to be eliminated. The homes and other properties within the mine fire zone were to be purchased. Then, the coal underneath could be removed and hauled away. This coal was sold to Hudson Coal Company and later to Glen Alden Coal Company that bought out Hudson Coal. The company receiving the stripped materials would retain the useable coal for sale. Hudson Coal (and later Glen Alden Coal) paid Carbondale Coal Company a profit from this sale.

In return for being allowed to strip mine the area, the Carbondale Coal Company, which got the mine fire contract, would dig out the fire and refill the land. Carbondale Coal would agree to pay a small royalty on the coal it removed to help defray the cost of acquiring and clearing the land. The coal company estimated that its costs would be about $12 million for digging out the coal and refilling the pits. It estimated further that it would get $13 million dollars worth of coal for a profit of about one million dollars. It expected to pay out about $500,000 in royalties.[28]

According to plan, the Redevelopment Authority would condemn the entire 130-acre tract it identified as the mine fire zone, purchase the homes, and demolish them. Then the Carbondale Coal Company would start stripping. In 1956, the dig-out was expected to take about three years, but it extended into the 1960s. Delays let the fire spread another five hundred to six hundred feet beyond the original perimeters, which increased costs and necessitated the seeking of additional federal and state funds.[29]

Many West Siders felt that there should be another way to get rid of the fire without taking their homes and properties, estimated to be worth about $2 million in 1956.[30] But virtually all the city's officials disagreed with them. C. B. Tomaine, chairman of the Redevelopment Authority, said that there was no other way. "That fire," he said, "is a cancer. You've got to go in and dig it out. If you get it all, it's done. If you don't, there's no telling where it will break out."[31] The Redevelopment Authority tried to soften the blow by developing a long-range plan to "rehabilitate" the area by building both residential and industrial sites on the reclaimed land after the fire was eradicated. Planners informed West Siders that one day they would be able to return to the area.

The dig-out of Carbondale's West Side mine fire began as a result of the city receiving federal funds under slum-clearance legislation. This meant that the West Side region was declared a slum. The Carbondale Redevelopment Authority then began buying, demolishing, and burning the condemned homes in the fire zone. By the end of 1960, it had condemned and purchased the first sections of land, and residents began to move.[32] However, it would take several years to clear the region completely of its residents.

A housing authority was set up to assist those who qualified for public housing, which involved some newly built duplex houses built for the displaced. But the term *public housing* carried a stigma of poverty, so most West Siders would not consider this option. In addition, the public housing projects seemed to be poorly built and skimpy, with little or no private land. To West Siders, this was not at all a good trade for their beloved homes.

The entire process of buying up West Side properties and relocating the residents was so slow and acrimonious that most of the residents were still in their homes waiting for offers from the Redevelopment Authority and pondering what lay ahead when the actual digging out of the fire began in January of 1961. But living in their beloved homes was about to become a nightmare worse than anyone could have imagined.

The Ultimate Horror

For the West Siders, life as they had known it was over, replaced by a daily, even hourly, struggle with the dig-out. As many continued to live in their homes, surrounded by the noise and dirt of the dig-out, they witnessed the daily work of crews digging out the fire, recovering the coal, and destroying unoccupied homes and other buildings as they dug from one area to another in the condemned zone.

Work crews, steam shovels, and huge drag lines that destroyed houses and tore into the earth were all around them. Those forced by circumstances to remain in their homes tell of watching as mining crews bulldozed or burned the homes of relatives and neighbors, stores and small businesses, and the two public schools that had been purchased for the dig-out. By the time the digging began, West Siders had been living with danger and difficulty for years. The dig-out, however, became the ultimate horror. Roads that had crisscrossed the region disappeared, replaced by enormous canyons exposing layer upon layer of rock, coal, and dirt. Clamorous steam shovels, trucks, and other machinery used by mining crews kicked up dust, dirt, and mud. Many residents interviewed for this study remarked that they would never forget the experience; more than forty years later they vividly remember the destruction. Several spoke of a particular memory, such as the day a certain home or group of homes were unceremoniously ripped apart or simply smashed by huge machinery.

"I saw the Collins home [the John Collins home on South Hospital Street] ," said Mary Purcell, a neighbor who lived up the street, "the morning they pushed it into a pit. I wish I'd never seen that."[33] Mrs. Gabriel (Helen) Costanzo told of the dirt and mud everywhere. In order to walk to town, she was forced to wear boots because of the deep mud—a result of the digging and flushing.[34] Another resident said his sister, living in one of the last homes left standing, was only able to get water by way of hoses because the water pipes on the West Side had been cut by that time.[35]

"A PART OF THE WEST SIDE NEIGHBORHOOD" – COURTESY OF ANGELO MAZZA

"Digging Out a Neighborhood" –
Courtesy of Angelo Mazza

"Dig Out Pit Near West Side Homes" –
Courtesy of Angelo Mazza

"Dig Out Scene" –
Courtesy of Angelo Mazza

"Equipment 1" –
Courtesy of Carbondale Historical Society

"Equipment 2" –
Courtesy of Carbondale Historical Society

"Equipment 3" –
Courtesy of Carbondale Historical Society

"Equipment 4" –
Courtesy of Carbondale Historical Society

"Equipment 5" –
Courtesy of Carbondale Historical Society

"EQUIPMENT 6" –
COURTESY OF CARBONDALE HISTORICAL SOCIETY

"EQUIPMENT 7" –
COURTESY OF CARBONDALE HISTORICAL SOCIETY

"EQUIPMENT 8" –
COURTESY OF CARBONDALE HISTORICAL SOCIETY

"EQUIPMENT 9" –
COURTESY OF CARBONDALE HISTORICAL SOCIETY

"EQUIPMENT 10" –
COURTESY OF CARBONDALE HISTORICAL SOCIETY

"EQUIPMENT 11" –
COURTESY OF CARBONDALE HISTORICAL SOCIETY

"Equipment 12" –
Courtesy of Carbondale Historical Society

"Equipment 13" –
Courtesy of Carbondale Historical Society

"Equipment 14" –
Courtesy of Carbondale Historical Society

"Homes on the Edge of a Dig Out Pit" –
Courtesy of Angelo Mazza

"Houses on the Edge of Abyss" –
Courtesy of Angelo Mazza

"Steam Shovel in a Major Cut – Note Homes Above" –
Courtesy of Angelo Mazza

"Steam Shovel" –
Courtesy of Angelo Mazza

Although all who had been and continued to live under these conditions were affected by the sheer horror of the situation, the women who were homemakers were particularly angered and frustrated by the realization that nothing they did would stop the dirt, noise, and overall disorder that now prevailed in their everyday lives. Ed Spall, writing in 2008, said he recalled that "Mom's biggest issue was the increased amount of cleaning necessary due to the dirt and mud stirred up and tracked around by the flushing operations in our yard and in the neighborhood. In our yard, she also struggled with a loss of clothesline space because the drilling equipment and trucks caused us to have to remove most of the lines to allow them to move around . . . also the dust would get on the drying clothes . . . this went on for about a year as I recall."[36]

Other women expressed the same memories of themselves or their mothers attempting to cope with the near-impossibility of keeping their homes clean and orderly while living with the mine fire. Mrs. Costanzo felt she was living a nightmare, her well-kept
But as bad as the dust and dirt might have been, the real horror of

bungalow off Scott Street surrounded by smoke, dust, noise, and mud.[37] Mrs. Madeline (Cooper) Purcell, who lived on South Hospital Street in a home that was one of the last to be purchased and destroyed, said that she and her female neighbors keep dusting and dusting but no matter what they did, the dirt never stopped coming into the home—through cracks in the surface or from the outside on the family member's shoes.[38]

The noise from the steam shovels, located across the street from Mrs. Purcell's home was unbearable, and seemed to never stop, she remembered. In fact, South Hospital Street, the area where the Cooper–Purcell home was located, was across the street from Sandy's Field. Once a large grassy area where children played and carnivals set up in bygone days, this had been a coal mine stripping site of Carbondale Coal Company since the early 1950s—some time before the dig-out commenced. During the dig-out, this area was part of the outer eastern perimeter of the mine fire zone. People living along South Hospital Street and the several side streets that connected with it were used to the noise, dirt, and constant truck traffic of the stripping pits. But it had been nothing, said Mrs. Purcell, compared to the period of the dig-out.[39]

"NIGHT TIME ON THE DIGOUT" –
COURTESY OF ANGELO MAZZA

AT HEIGHT OF FIRE — Vacant house in West Side redevelopment area formerly occupied by Patrick F. Caviston Jr. and family is shown as fire which destroyed it Monday afternoon was at its height. House and garage-workshop were destroyed. Next door house 81 Hospital, formerly occupied by Ambrose O'Rourke and family, was damaged. Two other fires occurred Monday. Extensive damage was caused to the William Colligan home at 166 S. Church St. The second was a minor fire in the second floor apartment of Edith Van Bergen, 69 Salem Ave. (NEWS photo by Mike Zrowka).

"Burning Deserted Home Purchased by Redevelopment Association" – Courtesy of Angelo Mazza

MINE FIRE PIT FLOODED—Thousands of gallons of waters from rampaging Fallbrook Creek Saturday broke through a makeshift dike to flood the "North Cut" of the Gillen Coal Mining Co. at the Carbondale mine fire. A big power shovel that had been working the pit located near N. Scott St. is completely covered. The shovel would be seen in the left foreground in above picture. Authorities estimated that depth of water is now more than 70 feet and is seeping into old mine workings.—(Scrantonian Photo by Ed Smith)

"Mine Fire Pit Flooded" – Courtesy of Angelo Mazza

"Scene at Digout" –
Courtesy of Angelo Mazza

Section of Digout Pit" –
Courtesy of Angelo Mazza

"STEAM FROM THE PIT" " –
COURTESY OF ANGELO MAZZA

the dig-out was the blasting. Work crews had to dynamite away sections of the diggings to get at coal beds or bring down rock and coal formations that were blocking access for the steam shovels and drag lines. As Mrs. Purcell described it, "men would come to your door and tell you that they were going to blast at a particular time and to stay inside and get ready for it. We didn't know what to do first." Certainly, stay indoors, "be sure that the children were inside." Then what? Try to protect "your best china and other breakables. But what about the pipes, walls, and the exterior of the house? What could you do?"[40]

When the blast occurred, "dishes came off shelves; plaster came down; more cracks appeared all over the house."[41] The family, said Mrs. Purcell, was particularly afraid that their furnace would be destroyed—something that would have spelled near financial disaster for a working-class family living in that area at the time. Mrs. Purcell recalled that her brother, William Cooper, with whom the Purcell family lived, had just put up a new chimney and was "so proud" of it. The blasting destroyed it.[42]

Moving House—Literally

Mrs. Mary Kerins Tryon, who lived on Willow Avenue, a hilly street that ran perpendicular to Brooklyn Street (Route 6), near the southwestern perimeter of the dig-out, was not one to surrender easily to the mine fire or the dig-out. She loved the house that her father had built and in which she and her husband were now living and raising their family. Faced with the imminent loss of her home, Mrs. Tryon came up with an alternative. Her daughter, Rosemary Tryon Grizzanti, who was interviewed in 2009, remembers that her mother was an unusual woman for her time. A stay-at-home homemaker, she ran her household well and was not one to sit back and do nothing.

Mrs. Tryon heard or read about a company that physically moved houses from one location to another. Probably by consulting the phone book, she located a company in Binghamton, New York, that did this. She contacted the owner, Gary Van Buton, who came to Carbondale and discussed with her the possibility of moving the Kerins–Tryon home to another location. From the mover's perspective, it was doable.

First, however, Mrs. Tryon had to work this out with the Redevelopment Authority. According to Mrs. Grizzanti, this was not easy to do; the Authority wasn't interested in getting involved in anything that further complicated an already complicated redevelopment plan. How did she convince them to change their position? Her mother probably prayed a lot, said Mrs. Grizzanti, who was a child at the time. But she may have also contacted someone or some agency in the federal government—who or what that agency was, Mrs. Grizzanti does not recall. Whatever it took to change the Redevelopment Authority's mind, change it *did* because they finally consented to the move.

As recalled by Mrs. Grizzanti, the arrangement was that the Redevelopment Authority would purchase the home; the Tryon's would purchase another lot and build a foundation on it in preparation for the house; the Tryon's would then buy the home back and the home would then be moved to the new site. Mrs. Grizzanti did not recall the exact financial arrangements involved with this, but she said she believed that her mother must have broken even, or nearly so, on the transaction. The Kerins–Tryon house was moved in the winter of 1960. All went as planned. The mover promised that the move would be so smooth that Mrs. Tryon could leave her milk bottles on the porch and that when the move was completed the bottles would still be in place and upright. They were! The site selected by the Tryon's was on North Scott Street, out of the mine fire zone by several blocks but still on the West Side. As arranged, they purchased the lot and built a foundation on it—ready for their home.

As Mrs. Grizzanti recalls it, the mover was very skilled. The original site of the Tryon house was on a steep hill at the top of Willow Avenue. The house had to be moved down the Willow Street hill, then taken along a discarded and derailed railroad bed where the Ontario and Western Railroad had run, across a railroad bridge, and along lower Scott Street to North Scott Street to the Tryon's new location. Mrs. Grizzanti said that the mover had had some problem with the utility lines during the move but got through nonetheless. Her mother, she said, was glad she had done this and the family settled in to their new location in their own house.[43] Mrs. Grizzanti and her husband live in that home today.

Inspired by Mrs. Tryon's success, another family also moved their house. Mr. and Mrs. Gabriel Costanzo lived off Scott Street in the fire zone. Not only did they love their neat little bungalow house, they wanted to save their home because their legally blind son knew the house so well and was comfortable there. Mrs. Costanzo contacted Mrs. Tryon, who encouraged her to speak with the Redevelopment Authority and emphasize the child's needs. The authority reluctantly agreed to allow the Costanzos to move their home as well. More West Siders were interested in following Mrs. Tryons and Mrs. Costanzo's ideas but the Redevelopment Authority called a halt to this—probably, said Mrs. Grizzanti, due to the paperwork involved or some other complications the authority did not want to take on.[44]

Most West Side residents of the mine fire appear to have been more complacent than either Mrs. Tryon or Mrs. Costanzo. But this was not totally the case. Many persons interviewed for this study recall that they or their parents contacted Carbondale city authorities, the mayor, city council members, the police, as well as officials and staff of the Redevelopment Authority, on numerous occasions to complain about conditions in the zone or to ask for help in making decisions about moving, or questioning the amount of money they were offered for their homes. According to several, many thought about moving their houses as Mrs. Tryon and the Constanzos had, but following these two moves, the Redevelopment Authority notified all mine fire zone homeowners that moving houses was not an option. So West Side residents remained in homes surrounded by a neighborhood that came to resemble a war zone.

"BOTTOM AND THIRD BEDS OF COAL OPPOSITE LOOKING CROSSING" – COURTESY OF CARBONDALE HISTORICAL SOCIETY

"Diggings 1950" –
Courtesy of Carbondale Historical Society

"Equipment Idle 1950" –
Courtesy of Carbondale Historical Society

"Gordon Avenue Loading Coal" –
Courtesy of Carbondale Historical Society

"Loading Gravel in Back of Gordon Avenue 1952" –
Courtesy of Carbondale Historical Society

"Looking Northwest Toward Pike Street" –
Courtesy of Carbondale Historical Society

"Mine Fire Digging Cut 1952" –
Courtesy of Carbondale Historical Society

"Mine Fire Digging" –
Courtesy of Carbondale Historical Society

"Overburden Cut 1950" –
Courtesy of Carbondale Historical Society

"Rock Dump 1950" –
Courtesy of Carbondale Historical Society

"Rock Dump and Cut 1952" –
Courtesy of Carbondale Historical Society

"Sandys Field" –
Courtesy of Carbondale Historical Society

After waiting to be contacted by the Redevelopment Authority with offers on their properties, most residents were shocked and dismayed by the amounts they were offered for their homes. Most offers were far too low to purchase another home. A Housing Authority had been created as a division of the Redevelopment Authority and was charged with helping residents of the fire zone relocate. But most people do not recall receiving any assistance from this agency beyond the offer to relocate into public housing—something that few of these proud, independent-minded people did.

West Siders were faced with the dismal fact that they were literally on their own for finding a new place to live. Most West Side residents still feel that there were no adequate provisions made for them to relocate. This feeling was reinforced by the paltry amounts of money offered for their properties—"way below market value," said one former resident. "We were offered an amount that wouldn't begin to buy a house somewhere else in Carbondale or that was enough to allow us to build a new home."[45] Said two former residents, "We had to move. There was nothing we could do. We looked at many properties, even in Jermyn (a neighboring community) and then decided to build (outside Carbondale)."[46]

Most West Siders were faced with the need to either borrow money or tap their savings to have a new home. But many did not want to pursue either option—the elderly people living on modest pensions and savings had been homeowners who were free of debt. Not only could they little afford to take out a mortgage, they were scrupulous about money matters and did not borrow or engage in financial dealings that might cause them hardship. As one resident put it, "All we had was our home."[47]

However, John Baldi, who was engaged by an urban renewal consulting firm to conduct relocation interviews with the families set for removal, says that the city made an effort to locate housing for West Side residents by asking the Carbondale Postmaster to enlist the help of mailmen who delivered residential mail throughout the city. Mailmen were to identify vacant houses or apartments and pass this information to the renewal authorities. In this way, lists of available housing were passed along to relocating West Siders.[48] When asked about this assistance, however, West Siders said they either had no knowledge of such lists or that they did recall lists but that the properties listed were either "shacks" or their prices had been "deliberately" inflated beyond a reasonable range.[49]

Some residents chose to stand firm, to refuse the Redevelopment Authority's first purchase offer. A few hired lawyers to represent them. First offers were very low—in the neighborhood of $3,000 to $5,000 as a result of the designation of the area as a "slum." Later, thanks to a successful legal appeal, realtors representing the Redevelopment Authority made slightly higher offers that were supposed to represent true market value. But, said one West Sider, the difference was often only a thousand or so dollars more and, if one had to hire a lawyer to negotiate, that expense took away significantly from any gain. Most West Siders interviewed for this study lamented the prices they had received for their homes.[50]

Other than the two residents who were able to negotiate for the moving of their houses, everyone eventually sold out. "What else could we do? There was no one who seemed to care about what was happening to us," said one West Sider.[51] Indeed, surrounded by the dismal and dangerous landscape of the mine fire zone, the people of the West Side seemed like a lost, forlorn people, left to fend for themselves.

The Redevelopment Authority was condemning and purchasing all the properties involved in the fire zone. With nothing to keep them there amid the muck and destruction, with only intermittent running water and sewerage, and with the daily onslaught of dirt and dust dredged up from the digging, residents moved out soon after their homes were purchased. They left behind not only their houses and the precious gardens and yards where they had so carefully nurtured shrubs, trees, flowers, and food for their tables, but a place and a way of life they loved and would never forget. Mine fire zone residents were allowed to take moveable parts from the houses, but it was impossible to remove larger items, such as fixtures, staircases and the like. Some people dug up prized plants or bushes, but most had to be left behind. Stories abound about nonresidents swarming over abandoned properties, attempting to salvage valuables before the houses were destroyed by fire or bulldozer.

C. P. Gilmore, covering the story in 1963 for *The Saturday Evening Post*, wrote, "While most West Side houses have been demolished and giant holes now gape where they stood, some reminders of the past remain. Cellar doors of the few remaining homes are still unlocked for the inspector's visits. The house where the Collinses died still stands, decayed and desolate, windows like eyeholes in a skull. Cellars—minus their houses—dot the hillsides. Here and there a well-maintained home, still inhabited, stands out in strange contrast to the panorama of desolation. Neatly trimmed lawns and blooming flower beds seem out of place in the scarred landscape."[52]

Some West Siders were still not certain about the dig-out, and remained reluctant to go. "It's still really heartbreaking," said Mrs. Jennie Fortuner, "to pick up and leave after thirty years. . . . I raised my children in this home and now three of them are married and the other one is supposed to be married sometime next year. I wish I could stay here until then."[53] William Cooper still remained in his home in 1963 and was digging in his garden when he was interviewed by a reporter and said that he "didn't know if he would be there when the flowers he was planting came up," but he went on planting.[54]

Joseph Cerra was also interviewed in 1963. He was seventy years old and said that his wife's father had given him the land when he returned from military service in 1919; his mother gave him $5,000 and he built his house. "The place," he said, " is paid for and everything I thought was set. I can't go back to work now. But I can't get another house for what I'm getting for this one."[55]

Jim Collins said that he had lived in danger for so long that maybe West Siders were immune to fear. Jim, who had discovered the bodies of his aunt and uncle in their home, was one of the last residents in his area of the West Side. In 1963, he was still living in the house next door to theirs, and claimed the fire didn't affect him very much. "It's all right as long as you keep the windows open," he told an interviewer.[56]

Mrs. Santo Perri, in 1963, spoke of the scars that would remain in the hearts and minds of West Siders after the West Side was redeveloped. Already relocated, Mrs. Perri said her memories of living on the West Side were vivid. "We had to leave. The hole in the backyard kept getting bigger and moving toward the house. The children would wake up sick and vomiting from the gas. We had a beautiful big cat we raised from a kitten. One day we found her dead in the cellar. We lived in that house nineteen years and didn't want to leave. But no home was worth what we had to go through." "But," she added, "every once in a while we'd go over and look around where our house used to be—to torture ourselves, I guess. It was beautiful over there. I'll never forget it."[57]

An Awesome Spectacle

The dig-out itself was described in *Popular Science Monthly* in May 1960 as "an awesome spectacle with gigantic machines precariously clinging to the brink of chasms while they claw at the precipices, the shovels dug out and worked in and outside of huge trenches, each about 125–200 feet in depth and 250–300 feet in width, trenches big enough to bury a cargo ship, that chopped across the West Side project area."[58] Writer Martin Mann went on to describe a flooded pit bottom where workers were dropping burning coal in the water to cool it before hauling it away. Workers related their experiences working in such conditions: "I never believed the stuff would burn like that underground. Walking past the burning chambers is like walking past an open furnace. The heat hits you in the face."[59]

The trenches were located on the outer perimeters of the fire and were designed to cut off its spread. After each trench was dug out and the fire removed, it was refilled with dirt from the next trench as the digging moved inward on top of the fire. It was estimated at the time that a staggering four million cubic yards of earth would be removed.[60] Overburdens of rock and dirt atop the coal "is gouged out by enormous draglines—as big as houses with ten-ton toothed buckets dangling from boom[s] the size of a bridge."[61] Each dragline was operated by one man who "casually [used] hydraulic-control levers to scoop ten tons of rock."[62]

As described in *The Saturday Evening Post* in 1963, "The work scene is awesome. Men with giant shovels, bulldozers, and trucks are now swarming over the site. Before they are through, they will dig out an area almost a mile long and a half-mile wide down to bedrock—on the average, a hundred feet or more . . . (moving) more earth than the builders of the Panama Canal."[63]

There were pits "big enough to swallow a battleship. . . . Clouds of smoke billow out from the stripping. Flames leap in underground chambers revealed by the digging. Glowing coals cast an obscene crimson light over the area at night. The draglines cut and bite, tearing the hot coal from the earth. The smell of burning sulfur fills the air . . . ."[64]

As much coal as possible was removed in the operation. Often still burning, the coal and other debris, extracted by the Carbondale Coal Company, was cooled with water and trucked to a site some distance away to be sold to the Hudson Coal Company. Coal judged sellable was conveyed to breakers for sale, since the return on the coal was to pay for the city's portion of the project. The Hudson Coal Company (later Glen Alden Coal Company) , which owned the subsurface rights, was paid a royalty.

The fact that the coal companies were making money on the dig led many West Siders to believe that mining the coal for resale, rather than putting out the fire or helping them rebuild their lives, became the primary focus of the coal companies, the Redevelopment Authority, and the city leaders. Several expressed the opinion that the locations of the dig-out cuts were determined less by the fire underneath than by the likelihood of recovering a load of saleable coal.[65] But people who were connected with the removal project maintained otherwise, and in fact, records of the project show little in the way of profits from the dig. Others maintained that the removal and sale of coal from the West Side mine fire zone enabled the city to dig out the fire and any profit made on the operation by the coal companies was reasonable.[66]

The overall strategy to destroy the fire was to cut off the burning coal by digging a trench, three hundred feet wide, around the area. According to reports, this almost didn't work because, as the last cut on the area's eastern section was being made, the fire burst out and nearly broke through a cross-town seam into deposits under the business district and the eastside residential section of the city. Workmen, according to observers, stopped it twenty feet from this seam.[67] Following this near disaster, then Mayor Frank Howard said, "That sewed it up . . . until then, we weren't sure we had cut it off. . . . We were really holding our breaths until then. If the fire had got under the railroad track (the Delaware and Hudson Railroad track that separated the West Side of Carbondale from the downtown area and, beyond, the East Side), we would have really been in trouble. That was the boundary of the redevelopment area. If it passed the boundary, we weren't authorized to tear down buildings (in the downtown and on the East Side of the city) and go after it. By the time we could have gone through all the necessary red tape to clear the way, there's no telling where the fire would have been."[68]

"Mine Fire 1"–
Courtesy of Anthracite Heritage Museum, Scranton, PA

"Mine Fire 2"–
Courtesy of Anthracite Heritage Museum, Scranton, PA

"MINE FIRE 3"–
COURTESY OF ANTHRACITE HERITAGE MUSEUM, SCRANTON, PA

"MINE FIRE 4"–
OURTESY OF ANTHRACITE HERITAGE MUSEUM, SCRANTON, PA

"Mine Fire 5"–
Courtesy of Anthracite Heritage Museum, Scranton, PA

"Mine Fire 6"–
Courtesy of Anthracite Heritage Museum, Scranton, PA

"Mine Fire 7"–
Courtesy of Anthracite Heritage Museum, Scranton, PA

"Mine Fire 8"–
Courtesy of Anthracite Heritage Museum, Scranton, PA

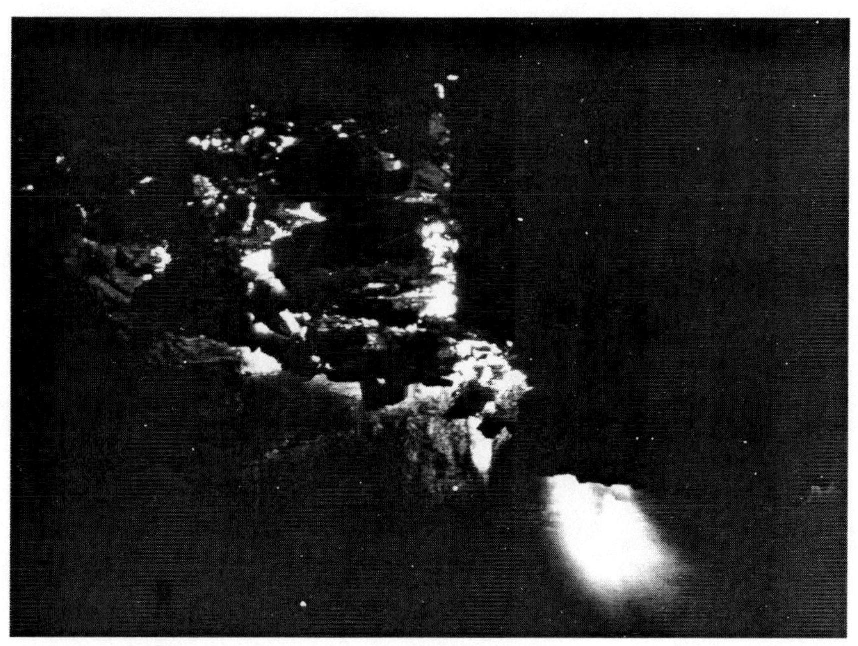

"Mine Fire 9"–
Courtesy of Anthracite Heritage Museum, Scranton, PA

"Mine Fire 10"–
Courtesy of Anthracite Heritage Museum, Scranton, PA

"Mine Fire 11"–
Courtesy of Anthracite Heritage Museum, Scranton, PA

"Mine Fire 12"–
Courtesy of Anthracite Heritage Museum, Scranton, PA

"Mine Fire 13"–
Courtesy of Anthracite Heritage Museum, Scranton, PA

"Mine Fire 14"–
Courtesy of Anthracite Heritage Museum, Scranton, PA

"Mine Fire 15"–
Courtesy of Anthracite Heritage Museum, Scranton, PA

Experts felt that the project could take as long as ten years to complete, including backfilling and reclamation. Others predicted that the job would be finished by 1968—two years ahead of schedule. In 1963, *The Saturday Evening Post* article by C. P. Gilmore reported that about 25 percent of the project had been completed.[69]

Meanwhile, city leaders promoted the idea that the day would come when the West Side region would be "reborn" according to the rehabilitation plan—with houses, maybe a ballpark, and an industrial park designed to attract new business to Carbondale. Thus, out of this bleak picture would come restoration and even prosperity for the Pioneer City. In 1957, the writer for *Pageant* was upbeat: "Every citizen of Carbondale is positive that the fire will be licked and prosperity regained. 'Like the phoenix,' said Mayor Kelly, 'we're going to come up out of our own ashes.'"[70]

Chapter 5:

Gone, But Not Forgotten

According to the records of the U.S. Bureau of Mines, work on the Carbondale Mine Fire Project was officially completed on July 24, 1972. It was one of the largest mine fire control projects undertaken under the Appalachian Regional Development Act of 1965. Total cost was $2.326 million. The project was said to have prevented the fire from spreading to nearby communities and involving some 100,000 people and more millions of dollars.[1]

Carbondale's Redevelopment Authority had implemented the mine fire project; this included redevelopment and recovery of the dig-out area after the mine fire was eradicated. To this end, the Redevelopment Authority prepared an Amended Urban Renewal Plan and Redevelopment Proposal that was accepted by the Carbondale City Council following a public meeting. The plan included a comprehensive redevelopment scheme that included residential, commercial, industrial, and recreational sites to be located in the restored mine fire zone.

To meet the need for residential property—the thinking was that West Side residents would want to move back after the fire was eradicated—about twenty-two acres in the redevelopment plan were set aside for residential housing: three neighborhoods designed for single-family homes with some two-family and multi-family lots or units here and there. According to the Redevelopment Authority records, each home lot was to be about 8,500 square feet—about 110 feet deep and 70 feet wide. Several recreational areas were to be provided for these new neighborhoods. The Redevelopment Authority would be responsible for providing streets, curbs, and the like.[2] Five parcels of land in the project were to be established for multi-family residential development—"garden-type" apartments or row houses of up to eight units per building, or twenty-five to forty units per parcel. These areas would likewise be supplied with recreational and other facilities.

Reporting on the progress of this plan in the 1972 edition of *PAHRA News* (published by the Pennsylvania Housing and Redevelopment Authority), the magazine said that "over the years it had become apparent that new industrial development" had to be created in the West Side Project area to "bring new life to the city."[3] Carbondale's Chamber of Commerce, the Carbondale Lackawanna Industrial Development Authority (CLIDCO), and the Lackawanna Council and Redevelopment Authority were united in this effort. A major part of the West Side mine fire redevelopment plan was to construct a commercial area near the city's downtown region that would attract residents for shopping. According to the PAHRA publication, the region north, west, and east of Carbondale contained "no significant shopping districts." It was estimated that about forty thousand people in this region would generate sales of over $100 million annually.[4]

The rebirth of the West Side offered city fathers and residents a real hope for the future of Carbondale; for some it was the first time since the coal industry went into decline that such a spirit existed. *The Saturday Evening Post* writer found optimism as well as tragedy in 1963: The town is stirring with new vigor. Business and civic groups are working to bring new industries to town and have several new plants to show for their efforts."[5] In the same article, the reporter interviewed Joseph Farrell, chairman of the Planning Commission, who said, "This used to be a good town. But with mining over, it was going downhill. Then strip mining came in and made a mess of it. Then this damn fire. Now that the battle has been won, we're ready to move. Now we've got citizen participation. The fire was the spark plug."[6] Mayor Howard enthusiastically echoed these sentiments: "The industrial site that we're going to build on the reconstituted fire area will be the salvation of this town. Carbondale is the city of the future.[7]

In the end, as city government leaders changed and Carbondale's economy continued down the slippery slope of economic decline, and as Carbondalians, particularly the young, moved out in search of their fortunes, the focus of city fathers and redevelopment leaders came to rest more on the creation of an industrial park than a residential village. More than one person believed that the modification of the original plan, which was to provide lots for homes and, thus, encourage former West Side residents (and others) to move there, was a factor in the further economic decline of the city to the present.[8] As a result of having removed so many West Siders from their homes to strip the mine fire, the city lost a huge tax base.

Although some evacuees did relocate in other parts of Carbondale, sometimes even on the untouched remaining area of the West Side, many more—and especially their children—moved away to neighboring communities and states. Instead, in order to attract industry to the reclamation site, city fathers offered attractive tax breaks that did not make up for the loss of taxes from West Side home and property owners. In the opinion of one resident, former West Siders would have returned to a rehabilitated West Side; he would have.[9] Other West Siders agreed; they would have returned to the West Side if given the opportunity.[10]

Today, Carbondale is vastly changed—demographically as well as physically—from the bustling little city that it was in the 1950s. The downtown area is attempting, under a new, younger administration to present the town in a new light to encourage business expansion and with it prosperity. Indeed, along the Main Street and streets adjacent to it there is some evidence of recovery. But at the same time there are many spaces where stores and businesses once thrived and few new businesses are to be found. The little city still shows great pride and its citizenry speaks with enthusiasm of various events planned to highlight the city; there is an impressive new library and several very good restaurants. The population has continued to decline, but there is a hopeful enthusiasm among Carbondalians that things are beginning to turn around.

The West Side still exists as a distinct, though no longer a particularly ethnic section of the city. It is still largely working-class.

The former mine fire zone is a large expanse that contains a strip mall, a public high school and elementary school, and a number of businesses.

Gone are the myriad of streets, alleys, courts, and avenues that dotted the old West Side from Brooklyn Street (which was reconfigured during the dig) to the remaining section of Hospital and Scott Streets. Former West Siders who had not seen this area since the mine fire would have a hard time determining exactly where their old homes had been. Landmarks, such as the view people who lived on South Hospital Street had of the City Hall clock are still there, but that street is no longer identified, and the entire location is much lower and flatter than it originally was because of the refilling and leveling. Nowhere in the mine fire zone is there anything left of the old West Side—no buildings, streets, or trees—nothing.

Interviewed in 1997, 1998, 2007, 2008, and 2009 about this era, West Siders looked back on the mine fire episode as a defining moment in their lives. Life, said several, was never the same again. Forty to fifty-plus years later, they readily acknowledged they still missed the West Side and the close family and neighborhood ties they had there. Several said their parents had never adjusted to relocation. At least three persons believed a father's or mother's death after moving was directly tied to the stress or sadness of separation from their beloved home and community.

The most overwhelming and constant memory of this period was of the horror of living in "the zone" and the helplessness of watching the destruction of their community. Every West Side resident interviewed for this study had clear personal memories of the dig-out period and the horror of living with the noise, dirt, fear, and uncertainty. Now, so many years later, many steadfastly maintained that the project leaders totally failed to take into account the real human suffering connected with the situation and that little or no consideration was shown them in their plight. Most stated that if the fire took place today, people would be less passive and submissive, that they would question and "stand up for their rights," but that, then, people like their parents were more submissive to authority and less educated. Consequently, they easily fell victim to the unfolding situation.[11]

The years of Carbondale's mine fire represent a major period in that city's history. For West Siders it represents sharp memories. In answer to the question, "Do you still see it (the West Side, your old neighborhood)?" all interviewed for this study said yes. Some, such as Mrs. Grizzanti, said she still remembers the streets—and even the cracks up and down them.[12] Interestingly, most of the people interviewed for this study in answering this question did not emphasize the mine fire or the difficulties related to it that they talked about earlier in the interview. Rather, to this question about remembering, they chose to relate fond happy memories of a special place—where they played, where their friends lived, what their houses were like and what they had in their gardens, who their neighbors were, and the like.

Some talked of remembering the fun they had growing up there, and expressed their sense of belonging to something special. "Gone," said one former West Sider, "but not forgotten—never."[13] "I close my eyes," another said, "and I can see it still."[14] "It will," added another, "never die as long as I live."[15] Perhaps this, then, is the final account of what the mine fire meant to all those who experienced it. The fire destroyed the West Side as it was, but the memories of West Siders keep it alive. So a vital though difficult and controversial phase in the history of Carbondale and Pennsylvania is preserved—as is the place West Siders called home—in the memories of those who lived through it.

Appendices

Carbon Monoxide Poisoning

Concentration of CO	Symptoms
35 ppm (0.0035%)	Headache and dizziness within six to eight hours of constant exposure
100 ppm (0.01%)	Slight headache within two to three hours
200 ppm (0.02%)	Slight headache within two to three hours; loss of judgment
400 ppm (0.04%)	Frontal headache within one to two hours
1,600 ppm (0.16%)	Dizziness, nausea, and convulsions within 45 minutes; insensible within two hours
3,200 ppm (0.32%)	Headache, dizziness and nausea within five to ten minutes; death within 30 minutes
6,400 ppm (0.645%)	Headache and dizziness within one to two minutes; death within 20 minutes
12,800 ppm (1.28%)	Unconsciousness after two or three breaths; death within three minutes

Table prepared by Michael C. Korb, January 15, 2009.

REPORT ON CARBONDALE MINE FIRE

During the summer of 1946 the City of Carbondale was negotiating with The Hudson Coal Company to secure a suitable location for a city ash dump. Before negotiations were completed and an agreement executed, the City of Carbondale proceeded to dump ashes and combustible material in the old Carey, Baxter & Kennedy stripping, without the knowledge or consent of The Hudson Coal Company. The Hudson Coal Company became aware that combustible material had been dumped and was afire at the above location about September 1, 1946 and brought this to the attention of the City in a letter from The Hudson Coal Company's Real Estate Agent, Mr. I. J. Evans, to Mayor Monahan, dated September 7, 1946. Copy of this letter was given to Mr. James F. Hunley, Mine Inspector, by Mr. C. Evans, Jr., President of The Hudson Coal Company on May 2, 1949.

The City attempted to extinguish the fire by using the regular city fire equipment but, after several days of unsuccessful effort, they withdrew. A shovel was moved in by The Hudson Coal Company to dig out the fire and, later on, the immediately affected area was blanketed with clay by the Company, but these efforts proved ineffective.

The Hon. Joseph J. Walsh, then Deputy Secretary of Mines, called a meeting in Harrisburg during 1949, which was attended by a group of State Mine Inspectors and U. S. Bureau of Mines representatives. Among the subjects discussed was the Carbondale Mine Fire.

The residents of the area and the City Officials were fearful that the fire would spread under the built-up sections of the City and called upon the Federal Bureau of Mines to make an investigation. Beginning in 1948, the U. S. Bureau of Mines, Pennsylvania Department of Mines and The Hudson Coal Company began to study the problem. A report submitted by Mr. S. H. Ash, Safety Branch,

- 2 -

U. S. Bureau of Mines, dated January 16, 1950, proposed a plan for the control of this fire. This plan consisted of an isolation cut and flushing of mine workings with silt, at an estimated cost of $336,258.

Before work could proceed, it became necessary to obtain trespass permits from various home-owners and, if stripping were to be done certain surface properties, necessarily, had to be acquired. This problem was placed before the City of Carbondale. The City Solicitor advised The Hudson Coal Company as to the estimated cost of acquiring individual properties for stripping purposes. The City of Carbondale claimed that it was financially unable to acquire the necessary properties at the estimated cost.

Since the fire was continuing to spread rapidly, it was essential that some method, other than stripping, should be started immediately to control the fire. It was then mutually agreed between the City of Carbondale, The Hudson Coal Company and the Federal Bureau of Mines, after numerous conferences with interested parties, that the plan of attack should consist of drilling boreholes from the surface to intersect the underground openings of the different coal beds, and of flushing silt into these openings. It was intended by these operations to control the fire by sealing underground openings.

While the negotiations were going on between the City and the Bureau of Mines, The Hudson Coal Company kept a continual watch on the area and noticed that the fire was progressing toward Fallbrook Creek and, a short time later, noticed steam and vapor on the East Side of Fallbrook. In order to determine to what extent the fire was progressing in the stripping fill, the Company drilled approximately 30 holes on the East Side of Fallbrook for the purpose of taking temperature readings and air samples.

- 3 -

The Bureau of Mines, in order to get started, agreed that the money expended by The Hudson Coal Company for the drilling of holes on the East Side of Fallbrook, and also for work done on the West Side of Fallbrook, could be applied toward the sponsor's share in lieu of the City's share in controlling the fire.

When the fire began to move toward The Hudson Coal Company workings on the West Side, holes were drilled in order to flush part of the area adjacent to Fallbrook and a stripping cut was started in order to cut out the fire in that area.

As of July 31, 1950, the Company had spent a total of $214,071.64 for the fire-control work on both sides of Fallbrook. The above expenditure is over and above the money received for the merchantable coal recovered by the Company from the fire-cut stripping. This drilling and flushing work has been carried on continuously by the Company and is still in progress.

Early in 1950 Federal Funds became available to carry on fire-control work. On June 6, 1950, a contractor, under the supervision of the U. S. Bureau of Mines, started this work, which consisted of drilling and flushing silt through the boreholes into the underground workings. The work continued until February 15, 1952. During this time the contractor drilled 199 boreholes and flushed 81,525 cubic yards of silt into the mine workings. This work was done at a cost to the Government of $106,758.26.

At the request of the Government Engineers, The Hudson Coal Company agreed to periodically patrol and take temperature readings in the general area and to send the Government a copy of the readings. Also, upon receipt of complaints from home-owners, the Company checked their cellars and installed small ventilating fans, where required, in an endeavor to keep the cellars clear of gases.

- 4 -

It tried to be helpful in this manner to the greatest possible extent.

At the request of Mayor Kelly and the City Council of Carbondale, a hearing was conducted in the C.Y.C. Building in Carbondale on January 14, 1953, at which time, in response to a request of the Mayor and City Solicitor, an effort was to be made by the U. S. Bureau of Mines, State Department of Mines, and The Hudson Coal Company to consolidate their studies and review the whole situation as a group rather than from independent angles, although all three of the above had been cooperating ever since the fire started. The Committee was convened by Mr. H. H. Otto on January 21, 1953, in The Hudson Coal Company Office, Scranton, Pennsylvania, at which time Mr. James F. Munley was made Chairman and Mr. Karl T. Miller, Secretary. The Committee consisted of the following personnel:-

The Pennsylvania Department of Mines:-
Messrs. James F. Munley, Mine Inspector, 1st Anthracite District
Theodore L. Wackley, Mine Inspector, 2nd " "
Theodore D. Rees, Mine Inspector, 5th " "
Charles Jones, First-Aid and Mine Rescue Instructor.

The Federal Bureau of Mines:-
Messrs. John W. Buch, Chief, Anthracite Sub-Region
John D. Cooner, Sr. Chief, Mining Branch, Anthra. Sub-Region

The Hudson Coal Company:-
Messrs. H. H. Otto, Assistant General Manager
K. T. Miller, Safety Engineer

Others who participated in the underground inspections were:-

The Hudson Coal Company:-
Messrs. J. Elvedge, Ventilation Inspector
A. Browning, Student
W. Devitt, Student
Gerald Blake, Asst. Supt.

Gillen Coal Company:- Mr. T. J. Gillen, Jr., Foreman

Surface inspections were started by the Committee on January 28, 1953.

Cellars were examined for carbon-monoxide and carbon-dioxide, with approved

- 5 -

types of detectors, in the general area in question. Sixty-one houses were examined, also two schoolhouses and the playground building on the site of the old hospital. In seven of the homes carbon-monoxide was detected in the cellars, and in some of the homes some carbon-dioxide was detected.

Five of the houses in which the carbon-monoxide was detected are located on Scott Street near the N.Y.O.&W. RR. crossing. The sixth house is at 47 Shall Avenue, also near the N.Y.O.&W. RR., but 300 feet northeast of the group of five. The seventh house is located on North Brooklyn Street, approximately 1200 feet southwest of the group of five as noted on Scott Street. This area where the carbon-monoxide was detected in the cellars is over an unflushed area.

No carbon-monoxide was detected during the investigation in homes overlying the area flushed by the Bureau of Mines. Previous to the flushing, gases (carbon-monoxide and carbon-dioxide) were detected in this area. This clearly indicates the beneficial effects of the flushing.

It is recommended, therefore, that flushing be continued as a possible means of eliminating these gases from within the homes in which it was detected during this investigation.

An underground investigation was made on February 10, 1953 by the Committee. The active workings of the Gillen Coal Company were inspected and no carbon-monoxide or carbon-dioxide were found. No carbon-monoxide was found by the party that traveled Counter "A" (shown on the accompanying map) until a point approximately 700 feet south of #3 Slope was reached. At this point there was an indication of carbon-monoxide and carbon-dioxide.

On the inspection of the old workings east of the watercourse, and up to the flushing at the foot of #3 Slope, no carbon-monoxide or carbon-dioxide was found. Along the perimeter of this flushing carbon-monoxide was detected.

- 6 -

These travelways are shown on the attached map, with legend denoting the presence or absence of carbon-monoxide.

The investigation was continued on February 11th by the Committee. The watercourse in the Bottom Bed and accessible places in the direction of Scott Street were traveled to a point near the intersection of Scott Street and the N.Y.O.&W. RR. crossing, where traces of carbon-monoxide were detected but no actual fire was visible. However, through a hole in the top coal, which was not accessible with equipment at hand, haze with an indication of smoke was noted. The committee members are of the opinion that further examination of this area would be too dangerous at this time.

CONCLUSIONS AND RECOMMENDATIONS

1. The flushing previously done has been effective in the area flushed and it is recommended that this be continued promptly wherever possible.

2. It is not practical to flood the area with water for the purpose of extinguishing the fire.

3. The most certain way of extinguishing the fire would be to dig it out, with the additional aid of flushing to retard the progress of the fire due to oxygen that might be fed to the fire by reason of a stripping cut. However, due to complications in securing surface rights, titles to all properties within the area, etc., the time element must be considered in any stripping excavation of the fire area.

- 7 -

4. Steps should be taken to make funds available for the continuance of drilling and flushing on the East Side of Fallbrook Creek, also downstream toward the N.Y.O.&W. Railroad bridge over the creek, in such a manner as to bridge the existing breach between the two areas of flushing.

5. Continuous steps should be taken on both sides of Fallbrook Creek to isolate and control the fire.

6. Provision should be made for periodic inspections, with temperature readings and air sampling, over such period of time as may be necessary.

Respectfully submitted by the Committee -

Representing the -

Pennsylvania Department of Mines (James F. Munley (Theodore L. Wachley (Theodore D. Rees (Charles W. Jones

U. S. Bureau of Mines (John M. Brach (John Doonan Jr

The Hudson Coal Company (H. H. Otto (K. T. Miller

Scranton, Pa.
March 12, 1953

Archbald Pa Nov. 14th 1953

To Hon. G E Smith Dep. Sec. of Mines
From James F Munley -- Mine Insp. 1st Dist.
Subject- - W.Carbondale Mine Fire

On November 12th 1953 in company with Chief of Police Francis P Judge of the City of Carbondale I made an inspection of the west Carbondale mine fire area and report as follows.

(1) The house at 78 Scott Street which at the time of the deaths of Mr. and Mrs. Patrick Collins of that address had been known as the occupied part of the No 78 house and the part which at that time was not occupied was known as the unoccupied part were inspected and of the Two sub-divisions the following is pertinent.

(A) That part of the house known as the occupied part has windows removed and fresh air is freely admitted . because of this condition no tests were made for Carbon Monoxide or Carbon Dioxide.

(B) That part of the house known as the unoccupied part was closed and tests for Carbon Monoxide was made in the kitchen part where XXXXXX .008 C.O. was indicated on the Colometeric testing instrument, also the floor and ceiling have been buckled and are in very poor condition. Temperature inside was 78 degrees F and on the outside it was about 45 degrees F

(2) No tests were made at the Mahoney house on N. Scott Street as no one seemed to be at home there.
Tests for Carbon Monoxide was made at No 70 Scott Street in the cellar of this house and there was no register to indicate Carbon Monoxide, tests were also made in a pipe which was driven into the surface on the side of the house and in this location .01 Carbon Monoxide was indicated on the Colorometric testing instrument. The Hudson coal company employees have placed an electric fan in the cellar of this house and this was in operation at this time.

(3) On the East bank of Fallbrook creek the surface area is very dry indicating heat has melted the snow which has recently fell in this area of North Scott Street where a dirt fill was placed over the area to assist in combating the mine fire .

(4) Several houses in the area of Scott and North Scott Streets from the N.Y.O.& W railroad tracks to the Mahoney house have been affected by subsidence , repairs to some of these houses was being made at the time of this inspection.

(5) No further work was being done at this time by Contractors for the Federal Bureau of Mines to affect the fire area.

Very Truly Yours
James F. Munley
James F Munley
166 Spruce Street
Archbald Pa.

RECEIVED NOV 23 1953 DEPARTMENT OF MINES

- 2 -

On Friday, November 14, 1952 about 11:30 A.M. Mr. James Collins of 82 Scott Street, Carbondale, Pa. went to visit his uncle and aunt, Mr. & Mrs. Patrick Collins, at their home at 78 Scott Street, Carbondale, Pa. He was concerned about the welfare of the above named relatives because they had not been seen about their home or premises in the usual manner. His fears were further aroused when, upon reaching the home, there was no response to his calls or to his request for admittance. He then entered the home to ascertain the whereabouts of his relatives. After searching around the home he found the dead bodies of Mr. & Mrs. Collins in a bedroom on the second floor. The body of Mr. Collins was found on the bed and that of Mrs. Collins lay on the floor near the bed.

One window in the above named bedroom was raised about 3½ inches from the bottom when Mr. James Collins entered the room, he immediately raised the window to a height of about 8 inches. He then went to an adjoining bedroom and raised the window in this room to a height of 8 inches. He then hurriedly called to some neighbors to inform them of what had happened and then notified Mr. Francis P. Judge, Chief of Police of the City of Carbondale and Dr. Charles Speicher, Deputy Coroner of Lackawanna County.

The Deputy Coroner conducted an investigation and made his report to the Carbondale Chief of Police, Mr. Francis P. Judge. He said that the death of Mr. & Mrs. Patrick Collins was due to coal gas fumes and that death had occurred about 18 hours previous to the finding of the bodies by Mr. James Collins.

The Hudson Coal Company officials were also notified of the tragedy and together with Mr. E. C. McCleary, Area Engineer of the Federal Bureau of Mines, his assistant, Mr. Charles Weber, made certain tests at the home at 78 Scott Street and about the premises. These tests were reported to Police Chief Judge as indicating .02% carbon monoxide in the bedroom where the bodies were found and comparable amounts in other parts of the premises.

Local newspapers and radio stations gave an account of the deaths herein mentioned and it was through this medium that the local State Mine Inspector, Mr. James F. Munley, learned what had happened. He contacted Mr. William J. Clements, Deputy Secretary of Mines of the Commonwealth of Pennsylvania, and advised him of the matter. Deputy Secretary Clements ordered an investigation by Mr. James F. Munley and told him to secure the assistance of the following: Mr. T. L. Wackley, Mine Inspector, Pa. Dept. of Mines, Mr. T. D. Rees, Mine Inspector, Pa. Dept. of Mines, Mr. Charles Jones, Mine Rescue Instructor, Pa. Dept. of Mines. Mr. Munley then contacted the Carbondale Dhief of Police to ascertain conditions and to inquire as to when the house at 78 Scott Street could be intered. He was advised that the house was sealed off and would remain so until Monday, November 17, 1952 when further tests were contemplated by the Hudson Coal Company and the Federal Bureau of Mines as well as the City of Carbondale authorities.

- 3 -

According to the direction of the Carbondale Chief of Police, the Inspectors named by the Deputy Secretary William J. Clements, went to the Collins' home at 9:00 A.M. on November 17, 1952 and met with the following officials of the Hudson Coal Company: Mr. John Reed, Mr. K. T. Miller, Mr. Fred Zollinger, Mr. Arthur Hand, Mr. James Elvidge, Mr. Joseph Rouland and Mr. Walter Petsold. Chief of Police Judge opened the door of the house at 78 Scott Street, Carbondale and the above named persons entered and made tests for carbon monoxide. During these tests the personel making same entered and left the house, thereby opening and closing doors in the process. At about 11:00 A.M. on this date about 25 tests had been made and the indication of these tests which were agreed to by all present during the testing was the following percentages of carbon monoxide.

LOCATION OF TEST	PERCENT OF CARBON MONOXIDE
Cellar of house	.01%
First Floor of house	.01%
Bedroom in which deaths occurred	.02%

Two air samples were taken by the representatives of the Penna. Dept. of Mines and these were analyzed by Anthracite Mine Inspector Andrew Wilson. The purpose of this was to find the content of oxygen and that of carbon dioxide. The analyses indicated the following:

LOCATION WHERE SAMPLE WAS TAKEN	PERCENTAGES INDICATED	
	Oxygen	Carbon Dioxide
Bedroom of house	20.35%	0.20%
First floor of house	20.65%	0.20%

The following pertinent conditions were noted:

A. No fires were burning in the house. The house contained two firing units, namely, the kitchen range and the furnace in the cellar. The fires in both units were extinguished when James Collins entered the house on November 14 and found the dead bodies of his uncle and aunt, Mr. & Mrs. Patrick Collins. From that date to November 17 there was no fire in the heating units.

B. Some unburned coal was in evidence in the firing pot of the kitchen stove and the cellar furnace firing unit also held a small amount of unburned coal. Both units were fired with Anthracite coal the last time they were attended.

C. Two small windows in the cellar, both in the immediate vicinity of the furnace, had a small opening in each. The windows had evidently been in this condition for a considerable time and were

- 4 -

not disturbed nor furthur considered in the process of testing for carbon monoxide.

D. The temperature in the kitchen of the house was 46 degrees Fahrenheit.

NOTE: A plan drawing of the house is attached to indicate locations.

At about 11:15 A.M. on November 17, 1952, it was agreed by all persons involved in the testing process to air the house,-that is, to ventilate it by opening doors and windows and to leave same in these positions until there would be no indication of the presence of carbon monoxide gas registered on the testing machines used for this purpose. This was done and on the same day at 1:15 P.M. the investigators again entered the house and made tests which showed that the cellar and the first floor (kitchen) were clear of carbon monoxide. After waiting until about 2:00 P.M. more tests were taken and it was indicated then that the bedroom was also clear. At this time it was agreed by all investigators to again shut up the house and leave it thus until November 19, at which time more tests for carbon monoxide and for hydrogen sulphide would be made.

On November 19 the following persons participated in the testing:

Mr. James F. Munley, Mine Inspector, 1st Anthracite District
Mr. T. L. Wackley " 2nd " "
Mr. T. D. Rees " 5th " "
Mr. Charles Jones, Mine Rescue Instructor, " Division

Mr. E. C. McCleary of the Federal Bureau of Mines
Mr. Charles Weber, Assistant to Mr. McCleary

Mr. John Reed, Hudson Coal Company
Mr. K. T. Miller, "
Mr. Francis Judge, Chief of Police of Carbondale
Mr. Frank Kelly, Mayor of the City of Carbondale

These tests indicated the following:

TEST MADE	PERCENTAGE INDICATED
Hydrogen Sulphide	Zero
Carbon Monoxide - in cellar of house	.015% to .025%
" " - on first floor	.01%
" " - in bedroom	.016%
" " - in surface crack in garden	.01%
" " - along cellar wall, outside	.0025%

- 5 -

While these tests were being made other families living in the immediate area called on the Hudson Coal Company officials to make XXXXX tests in their homes. These tests were made and the results were reported verbally as containing small percentages of carbon monoxide.

The representatives of the Pa. Dept. of Mines decided to make further tests with a greater lapse of time intervening than in the previous tests. It was agreed that these tests would be made on November 26, 1952 at 10:00 A,M. and Chief of Police Judge of Carbondale was requested to seal off the house until that date.

These tests were made and the results as indicated on the carbon monoxide testing machine were witnessed by the following personel:

James F. Munley, Mine Inspector, 1st District
T. L. Wackley, " 2nd "
T. D. Rees, " 5th "
Charles Jones, Mine Rescue Instructor, Pa. Dept. Of Mines
Francis Judge, Chief of Police, Carbondale
Frank Kelly, Mayor, Carbondale
Ray Schrader, Superintendent, Gas & Water Company

The results indicated by the machine were as follows:

LOCATION WHERE TESTS WERE MADE	TIME November 26	PERCENT OF CARBON MONOXIDE INDICATED
Kitchen of house	10:20 A.M.	0.017%
Bedroom where death occurred	10:30 A.M.	0.017
Attic of house	10:40 A.M.	Zero
Upstairs unoccupied	10:45 A.M.	Zero
Cellar - near boiler	10:55 A.M.	0.02
Rear lid right side kitchen stove	11:00 A.M.	0.01

The house at 78 Scott Street, Carbondale, Pa. is in the relative immediate area of what has been generally referred to as the Carbondale West Side Mine Fire. Here during the years of 1950 and 1951, the Federal Bureau of Mines officials have supervised the drilling and the flushing of certain bore holes drilled into the workings of the Hudson Coal Company in this area. They have also supervised the placing of inert materials over the surface area. After a considerable amount of this work was done the Federal Bureau of Mine officials reported to the Honorable William Monahan, who was then Mayor of Carbondale, that the fire was out. Later, an article appeared in the "Polular Mechanics" magazine to the effect that the Carbondale mine fire was extinguished.

/6/

There is much heat coming to the surface from the underground in the XX vicinity of Scott Street and North Scott Street, Carbondale, Pa. and the inhabitants of homes in this area have expressed indignation aboutthis gas condition which they claim is caused by the mine fires near their homes. About 40 of those home owners have called on the Mayor of the City of Carbondale complaining bitterly and demanding relief from their sufferings caused by the gas which they claim to be in existence on their lands.

NOTE: Mine Inspectors James F. Munley, W. G. Ward and D. H. Connelly of the Pa. Dept. of Mines, together with Mr. S. H. Ash of the Federal Bureau of Mines made a study of the Carbondale West Side Mine Fire about the year 1949-1950. Their findings and report was the basis for an appropriation made to the Federal Bureau of Mines to fight this fire. Their report which is on file in the Dept. of Mines at Harrisburg, Pa. and at Washington, D. C. Federal Bureau of Mines is additional information relative to this present investigation.

Prints of the area of Scott Street and North Scott Street, Carbondale, showing surface features and underground features are attached, - the house at 78 Scott Street is colored in red.

Respectfully submitted

James F. Munley

James F. Munley, Mine Inspector
166 Spruce Street, Archbald, Pa.

Theodore L. Wackley

Theodore L. Wackley, Mine Inspector
1801 North Washington Ave., Scranton, Pa.

T. D. Rees.

T. D. Rees, Mine Inspector
R. D. Clarks Summit, Pa.

Charles W. Jones

Charles Jones, Mine Rescue Instructor
Girardville, Penna.

BERNARD HERMAN
41 ...

R E L E A S E

KNOW ALL MEN BY THESE PRESENTS, That

WHEREAS, a subsurface fire is presently burning in the coal beds underlying a certain area of surface land in Lackawanna County, Pennsylvania, within the City of Carbondale, as shown on a plat thereof hereto attached and made a part hereof, and

WHEREAS, The Commonwealth of Pennsylvania is willing to expend money and have certain work performed in attempting to halt the progress of said fire, bring the same under control, and extinguish same by sealing surface and underground openings to said fire and the surrounding area to prevent the passage of air thereto, and

WHEREAS, other persons, firms, corporations, or municipalities may cooperate and assist said Commonwealth of Pennsylvania in its attempt to bring said fire under control, and

WHEREAS, the undersigned are owners of property overlying part or parts of the area above mentioned.

NOW KNOW YE THAT we, the undersigned owners of property in the County of Lackawanna, Commonwealth of Pennsylvania, within the area aforesaid as shown on a plat thereof hereto attached, for and in consideration of the attempts to be made by the Commonwealth of Pennsylvania and those cooperating with and assisting it in bringing the fire above described under control and ultimately extinguishing the same, and in consideration of the benefits which may inure to us and in consideration of the execution of similar releases by other owners,

West Carbondale Mine Fire — Inspection of Houses in General Area

Weather Clear - Warm — Date March 27 1954

Time	Name	Address	% Gas C. O.	C. O.^{2}	Test by	Symbol	Fan in use
8:00 to 4:00	H. L. Christian	1 Brooklyn	.004 .002	C.	Ward and Wackley	A	No
	H. Martino	10 Hudson	.002 0 .002	C	Ward and Wackley	A	No
	A. Barbaro	20 Woodlawn	.002 0 .002	C	Ward and Wackley	A	Yes
	Mary Keegan	19 Woodlawn	.004 .002	C	Ward and Wackley	A	No
	J. Swartz	18 Woodlawn	.002 0 0	C	Ward and Wackley	A	No
	Langman	6 Hospital	.002 0 0	Trace	Ward and Wackley	A	No
	A. Ladoni	1 Hudson St.	.008 .001	C	Ward and Wackley	A	No
	Ladoni Gas Station		.001	C	Ward and Wackley	A	No
	M. Gonacci	14 Delaware	.001 0 0	C	Ward and Wackley	A	No
	C. Gonacci	15 Delaware	.001 0	C	Ward and Wackley	A	No
	Wm. Rosler	11 Delaware	.002 0 0	C	Ward and Wackley	A	No
	T. Kelly	13 Delaware	.002 0 0	C	Ward and Wackley	A	No
	L. Barbour	21 Woodlawn	.003 0	C	Ward and Wackley	A	No

March 27 cont'd. 4:00 to 12:00

AAA - Recommended that windows and doors be opened.

AAA^1 - Recommended that windows and doors be opened.

AAA^2 - Recommended that windows and doors be opened.

AAA^3 - Recommended that windows and doors be opened; and cracks in cellar be closed.

B - All clear except holes in cellar .04 CO.

B^1 - CO^2 - 4" about 9 feet along cellar floor.

B^2 - CO^2 at one spot - 4". Trace CO. Opened cellar door and windows.

B^3 - CO^2 - 4" on floor in coal bin about 3 feet along wall.

B^4 - Had children removed to another home for sleeping. .008 CO in bed rooms. All windows were opened wide and to return for later check.

B^5 - Windows were not open enough. Had windows in cellar and on all floors opened wide.

B^6 - CO^2 at hole.

B^7 - Condition improving; suggested windows be kept open wide as they were at time of second check. One room is to be used for sleeping, with a small fan to help circulation, in addition to open windows.

West Carbondale Mine Fire Inspection of Houses in Gen

Weather____________________ Date______________ 19__

Sheet 2 of report of March 13th to 19th inc.

Time	Name	Address	% Gas C.O	C.O.$_2$	Test by	Symbol	Fan in use
3/16/54	H Burke	36 Scott	.002		Black rdw		Yes
4 to 12	M Carroll	38 Scott	.Trace		Do		Yes
	W Cooper	57 S Hospital	.000	4"	Do	B 1	Yes
	P Kerins	65½ Willow	.002	4"	Do	B 2	Yes 2
	L Duffy	69 N Brooklyn	.004		Do	B 3	Yes 2
	J Bruno	67½ N Brooklyn	.002		Do		Yes
	J Symonies	72 N Brooklyn	.004		Do		No
3/17/54	K Spall	65 Willow	.001	Mackley	Ward &		No
	P Kerins	65½ Willow	.003	&	Black		Yes 2
	Bore Hole 21	rear 65 Willow	.1	Schrader	Do		open air top of h
	K Rabuck	57 Willow	.001	4"	Do		No
	D Heenan	42 Willow	.001		Do		No
	P Kane	70 Scott	.001		Do		Yes
	L Duffy	69 N Brooklyn	004		Do		Yes 2
	T Moylan	61 Scott	.001		Do		Yes 2
	H Downs	52 Willow	.000	4"	DO		No
	L Duffy	69 N Brooklyn	.002		Richards		Yes 2
	J Symonies	72 N Brooklyn	.Trace		Do		No
	H Burke	36 Scott	.001		Do		Yes
	M Carroll	38 Scott	.001		Do		Yes
	P Kerins	65½ Willow	.002	4"	Do		Yes 2
	W Cooper	57 S Hospital	.000	4"	Do		Yes
3/18/54	L Duffy	69 N Brooklyn	.002		Jones		Yes 2
	J Bruno	67½ N Brooklyn	.001		& Black		Yes
	J Sheridan	67 N Brooklyn	.002		Do		No
	J Symonies	72 N Brooklyn	.002		Do		No
	H Pinlon	53 N Brooklyn	.001		Do		No
	A Fontione	49 N Brooklyn	.001		Do		No
	A Riesen	45 Scott	.001		Do		Yes
	T Moylan	61 Scott	.002		Do	A3	Yes 2
	J Brunner	8 Ontario	.002		Do		No
	E Moylan	45 Scott	.001		Do		Yes
	P Kerins	65½ Willow	.001 and		Do		Yes 2
	P Kerins	65½ Willow	.1 in cellar		creek		
	P Kane	70 Scott	.001		Do		Yes
4 to 12	T Moylan	61 Scott	.000		Stack	B 1	Yes 2
	P Kerins	65½ Willow	.002		Do	B 2	Yes 2
	A Hordesky	55 Willow	.001		Do		No
	H Downs	52 Willow	.000		Do	B 3	No
	J Symonies	72 N Brooklyn	.000	Yes	Do	B 4	No
	J Ward	73 N Brooklyn	.Trace		Do	B 5	No
	L Duffy	69 N Brooklyn	.002		Do	B 6	Yes 2
	J Sheridan	67 N Brooklyn	.Trace		Do	B 7	No
	J Bruno	67½ N Brooklyn	.004		Do	B 8	Yes
	E Moylan	51 Devine	.001		Do	B 9	Yes
	H Burke	36 Scott	.000		Do	B10	Yes
	P Kane	70 Scott	.000		Do	B 11	Yes
	W Cooper	57 S Hospital	.000		Do	B 12	Yes
3/19/54	K Spall	65 Willow	.004		Black	A 1	No
8 to 4	P Kerins	65½ Willow	.004		Do	A 2	Yes 2
	P Kerins Bore Hole 21	65½ Willow	.1		Do		
	P Barrett	66 Willow	.001		Do		No
	A Hordesky	55 Willow	.003		Do		No
	C Berry	50 Willow	.001		Do		Yes
	Mrs. McGuirgan	53 Willow	.001		Do		No
	H Downs	52 Willow	.000	4"	Do		No
	John Gilroy	91 Scott	.000	Trace	Do		No
	A Germano	85 Scott	.000	4"	Do		No
	W Cooper	57 S Hospital	.000	Trace	Jones		Yes
	T Moylan	61 Scott	.002		Do		Yes 2
	P Kerins	65½ Willow	.003		Hanley		Yes 2
	L Duffy	69 N Brooklyn	.002		Mackley		Yes 2
	J Symonies	72 N Brooklyn	.004	Black &	Schrader	A3	No
	J Bruno	67½ N Brooklyn	.001		Do	A4	Yes
			.008				

Continued .5%

3/17/54

B1 Test for Carbon Monoxide at crack in washroom of cellar shows .5% Carbon Monoxide entering at this point . Test taken with Carbon Monoxide detector , recommended that cellar windows be opened full.

3/18/54

A1 Carbon Monoxide in .1% plus from crack in cellar floor ; all doors and windows ventilated.

A3 Carbon Monoxide test shows .1% plus and .04% in cracks in basement floor

A4 Carbon Dioxide in Kanes in twin holes in cellar floor.

B1 Basement clear traces C O in cracks in cellar floor , checked at fan on second visit

B2 .001 C O on first floor, except pantry which is .002 % Basement .002% C O is general. -- .1% C O from each of three holes along area of coal bin also Bore Hole No P 21 at rear of house shows .1% plus

B3 Carbon Dioxide shows 4" and 5" in small sections of cellar on three spots in line with sewer

B4 C O clear except at crack in floor .005" and at drain pipe .04" sealing recommended and fan recommended to be put in.

B5 Trace Co found on edge of coal bin.

B 6 Cracks in basement should be sealed. 1% Carbon Monoxide coming from cracks.

B7 Trace C O in basement

B8 Told to open windows , they complain of bore hole fumes from street location.

B 9 told to open windows in cellar to a greater extent.

B10 Hole in corner of cellar near fan has .01% Carbon Monoxide emitting.

B11 Holes and cracks in cellar have been sealed, -- .001 C O coming from bleeder pipe on N W Corner outside house.

B 12 4 inches of Carbon Dioxide from local spots in cellar.

3/19/54

A1 Carbon Dioxide traces all along cellar floor .

A2 .002 Carbon Monoxide in pantry and in bath room.

A3 .003 Carbon Monoxide in general area

.02 Carbon Monoxide coming from crack in floor.

.04% Carbon Monoxide coming from location of sewer in cellar

4" Carbon Dioxide coming from area of sewer in cellar, all windows and doors were closed, recommended opening of the windows and doors and waited until this was done, also recommended that a trap be put in sewer in cellar location.

A4 .008 Carbon Monoxide coming from crack in cellar floor and wall on west side of house.

REPORT ON
COAL MINE FIRE CONTROL PROJECT
CARBONDALE, LACKAWANNA COUNTY, PENNSYLVANIA

By

F. E. Griffith
Mining Engineer

and

E. P. Thomas
Resident Engineer

UNITED STATES
DEPARTMENT OF THE INTERIOR
BUREAU OF MINES

REPORT ON
COAL MINE FIRE CONTROL PROJECT
CARBONDALE, LACKAWANNA COUNTY, PENNSYLVANIA

By

F. E. Griffith
Mining Engineer

and

E. P. Thomas
Resident Engineer

INTRODUCTION

As the result of an act of Congress appropriating money for the control of mine fires in inactive coal deposits, the Director of the Bureau of Mines was authorized to prosecute projects in cooperation with other agencies, Federal, State, or private, for carrying on this work.

Several discussions and conferences were held with officials of the City of Carbondale, the Hudson Coal Company, and the Pennsylvania Department of Mines regarding the control of the fire burning in the abandoned inactive Powderly colliery at Carbondale, Lackawanna County, Pennsylvania. At the request of the City of Carbondale and the Hudson Coal Company, personnel of the Bureau of Mines made a survey of the involved area. Following these discussions and survey, the Bureau of Mines prepared plans and specifications for the control of the fire, sent out invitations to bid covering the proposed work, and awarded the contract to the lowest bidder, Timothy Burke, Inc., Scranton, Pa.

Work of controlling the fire west of Fall Brook Creek was carried on by the Hudson Coal Company, and the remaining control work east of the Fall Brook Creek was prosecuted by the Federal Government.

The total cost of the work done by the Federal Government through February 15, 1952, including 10 percent for supervision and administration, was $106,758.26. Through July 15, 1950, the Hudson Coal Company spent $214,071.64 on this fire, and work west of Fall Brook Creek was continuing at the time of the writing of this report.

ORIGIN AND HISTORY OF THE FIRE

In August 1946 a fire was started in an abandoned coal strip pit near the Fall Brook Creek on the west side of the City of Carbondale. The abandoned strip pit had been used as a garbage dump by the City of Carbondale for about 5 years, during which time it was ignited and, in turn, ignited discarded carbonaceous material in the spoil bank and the exposed coal beds along the highwall of the strip pit.

Approximately $1,500.00 was spent by officials of the City of Carbondale in an unsuccessful attempt to control and extinguish the fire. Large quantities of water were poured on the burning masses and small excavations were made at various locations, but the project was given up because of the lack of funds to continue the work.

Prior to starting and during the early stages of the work on this project, officials of the Hudson Coal Company reported that carbon monoxide and carbon dioxide were found in such quantities in the No. 7 slope area of the adjoining Coal Brook colliery that the workmen, from time to time, had to be withdrawn. It was believed that these gases came from the mine fire area through old abandoned workings.

The officials of the City and the coal company recognized the serious threat of this fire to life and health of residents in the immediate area, the danger of the fire spreading under a larger area of the City, and requested the Federal Government for assistance in its control.

In a report dated February 20, 1948, Mr. C. F. Weber of the Wilkes-Barre, Pa., office recommended that this coal mine fire be controlled.

A report submitted by Mr. S. H. Ash, dated January 16, 1950, proposed a plan for the control of this fire, which consisted of an isolation channel and flushing mine workings with incombustible silt, at an estimated cost of $336,258.00. Subsequent exploration and investigation indicated that the fire had spread more rapidly than had been anticipated which precluded the possibility of carrying this plan through to successful completion.

EXTENT OF THE FIRE

The fire area east of Fall Brook Creek covered approximately 15 acres. Four coal beds, namely the New County, Top Clark, Bottom Clark, and the Third, and carbonaceous material contained in the spoil bank were on fire at the time work was started by the Federal Government on this project.

The floor of the Third bed is approximately 100 feet below the surface.

A typical section of this area is as follows:

Description	Rock in ft.	Coal in ft.	Accumulated depth from surface in ft.
Surface wash	23		
Rock	15		38
New County bed		4	42
Separation rock	38		80
Top Clark bed		5	85
Separation rock	2		87
Bottom Clark bed		6	93
Separation rock	2		95
Third bed		5	100

PLAN OF OPERATIONS AND PRELIMINARY WORK

The plan of operations, which was finally decided upon after numerous conferences with interested parties, consisted of drilling boreholes from the surface to intersect the underground voids and openings of the different coal beds and flushing incombustible silt material into these voids and openings. It was intended by these operations to control the fire by sealing all the underground openings to exclude air from the fire.

Preliminary work consisted of the following:

1. Preparing and executing an agreement between the Federal Government and the Hudson Coal Company, outlining the work to be done by both the Federal Government and the Company and establishing suitable and legal means of financing the project. A copy of this agreement is appended.

2. Preparing and executing a form of release with all property owners in the area, permitting entrance on these properties for doing work on the project. A copy of this agreement is appended.

3. Assisting with the drafting of and obtaining a resolution, copy appended, from the City of Carbondale, permitting work to be done on the streets, walks, and roads and on other property owned by the City in connection with the control of the mine fire.

4. Obtaining cost figures of money expended by the Hudson Coal Company for work previously done in controlling the fire for which credit was subsequently allowed in the amount of $175,412.00.

It might be mentioned here that additional credit in the amount of $38,659.64 was allowed the Company during the fiscal year 1951.

5. Preparing the plans, specification, form of contract, and the invitation to bid papers. A copy of the specification and Exhibits A and B included in the invitation to bid are appended.

The invitations to bid were sent to the following prospective bidders on May 4, 1950:

John Booth, Inc., 17 Salem Avenue, Carbondale, Pa.
H. B. Sproul, contractor, 222 W. Olive Street, Scranton, Pa.
Timothy Burke, Inc., 1222 Marion Street, Scranton, Pa.
Perry Construction Co., 825 Olive Street, Scranton, Pa.
Sprague & Henwood, 222 W. Olive Street, Scranton, Pa.
Sweeney Brothers, 40 Poplar Street, Scranton, Pa.
Battle Brothers, 315 Genet Street, Scranton, Pa.
Gasparini Excavating Co., 1439 Main Street, Peckville, Pa.
Goering Construction Co., Inc., 65 E. Market St., Wilkes-Barre, Pa.
Ezra Stipp Construction Co., Love Road, Scranton, Pa.
Severin W. Sokol, Factoryville, Pa.
Wyoming Valley Equipment Co., 1089 Wyoming Avenue, Forty Fort, Pa.
B. G. Coon Construction Co., 278 Union Street, Luzerne, Pa.
Harris Walsh, Inc., 37 Lackawanna Avenue, Scranton, Pa.
W. F. McHenry, 677 Carey Avenue, Wilkes-Barre, Pa.
State Equipment Co., 642 Market Street, Kingston, Pa.
Tolerico Excavating Co., 404 Main Street, Simpson, Pa.
C. B. & M. Construction Co., 338 N. Broad Street, West Hazelton, Pa.
Scranton Line Construction Co., 1620 Adams Avenue, Scranton, Pa.

The sealed bids were opened at 2 p.m., May 19, 1950, in the office of the Mayor of Carbondale in City Hall, Carbondale, Pa. Those present at this time were Mayor William L. Monahan and City Solicitor James D. Stone representing the City of Carbondale; Mr. John M. Reid, general manager, and Mr. E. H. Lewis, mining engineer, representing the Hudson Coal Company; officials from Timothy Burke, Inc., Scranton, Pa., Severin Sokol, Factoryville, Pa., Gasparini Excavating Co., Peckville, Pa., and Tolerico Excavating Co., Simpson, Pa.; and Messrs. F. E. Griffith and E. P. Thomas representing the Bureau. An abstract of the bids received is appended. Mr. Griffith announced that Timothy Burke, Inc., was the lowest bidder. Mr. John M. Reid assured the officials that this company had the necessary equipment to perform the work outlined in the bid. At a later date the contract was awarded to Timothy Burke, Inc.

PROSECUTION AND NATURE OF THE WORK

Prior to the start of work by the contractor on June 6, 1950, the Government's resident engineer and engineers from the Hudson Coal Company studied all available mine maps of the inactive mine, consulted with former officials, and located borehole points on the surface. The area in relation to the City of Carbondale is shown in photograph No. 73910 appended.

The contractor's first work on the project consisted of drilling boreholes to intersect the burning mine workings. The location of the first hole drilled by the Government is shown by an arrow in the appended photograph No. 73908.

Equipment Used

The equipment used in these operations was as follows:

(a) two 6-inch churn drill rigs
(b) one D-7 angledozer
(c) six 10-ton trucks
(d) two gasoline-motor-driven water pumps
(e) two ejector boxes used for flushing

Photograph No. 75019, appended, shows a drill in operation, and photograph No. 75026, appended, shows an ejector box used for flushing operations. Photograph No. 77425, appended, shows the angledozer; photograph No. 77426, appended, shows smoke and fumes being emitted from a borehole during the process of drilling; and photograph No. 77427, appended, shows a truck unloading silt into the ejector box.

Drilling

The original contract called for the drilling of 65 boreholes. This number was subsequently changed by change order No. 1, copy appended, to extend the drilling to an estimated 125 boreholes. At a later date after it was determined to extend the work further, the contractor was instructed by letter, dated January 7, 1952, copy appended, to drill and flush additional boreholes located in the vicinity of the previous Hudson No. 8 borehole.

The entire drilling operations consisted of drilling 199 boreholes, most of which penetrated the lowest or Third coal bed. Many difficulties were encountered during these drilling operations in broken and caved ground. Two sets of drilling tools were wedged in the boreholes and could not be recovered. Drilling was especially slow and difficult where holes had to be drilled in loose, back-filled ground.

High tension electric power wires, city water mains, sewer systems, homes, fences, and outbuildings further complicated the drilling operations and the selection of borehole sites. Drilling progress was further hindered by steam, fumes, and gases being evolved from the boreholes, as can be observed from photograph No. 75025 appended.

Even though much care was given to selecting borehole sites, on several occasions the drill penetrated solid pillars of coal. In these cases charges of explosives were fired to blast the pillars and expose the underground voids. Map No. 1 appended shows the location on the surface where holes were drilled, and map No. 2 appended shows the area underground where the holes penetrated.

A total of 14,669 feet of borehole was drilled at a cost of $24,920.30.

Casing

All boreholes drilled were cased to varying depths depending upon the nature of the ground. The casing used varied from about 10 to 70 feet in length. The contract for doing this work required the contractor to provide new 6-inch casing at $2.00 per foot, install casing in boreholes at 50 cents per foot, and salvage the casing at the completion of the flushing operations at 10 cents per foot. For all of these operations, 2,939 feet of new casing was provided at a cost of $5,878.00; 4,069 feet of casing was installed at a cost of $2,034.50; and 1,260 feet of casing was salvaged at a cost of $126.00.

Because of caving of boreholes, earth movement, and breaking of the casing at joints, it was nearly impossible to salvage all of the casing during these operations. Upon the completion of all of the drilling operations, all of the casing, except that remaining in the 26 boreholes from which temperature readings and air samples are to be collected, was either lost in the boreholes or was of such short lengths that it had no further value. The short lengths of casing resulted from the necessity of cutting the casing off with an acetylene torch after being raised a short distance so that flushing could be carried on in higher levels. Photograph No. 77425, appended, shows the angledozer being used to salvage the casing in one of the boreholes.

Twenty-two holes, in which casing was left for temperature reading and sampling purposes, were capped in accordance with the specification, at a cost of $66.00. The four remaining holes used for this purpose were capped by a suitable means and provided gratis by the contractor.

Incombustible Flushing Material

A supply of an incombustible waste product, from a central coal cleaning and sizing breaker, was made available to the Government gratis by the Hudson Coal Company. This supply of flushing material was in a settling basin near Mayfield, Pa., about 5 miles from the site of the fire control project. Ten grab samples of the material were collected prior to starting work on the project. The samples were analyzed at the Bureau of Mines laboratories at Pittsburgh, Pa. The analyses showed the highest incombustible content to be 84.4 percent, the lowest 76.8 percent, and an average of 79.5 percent for the ten samples. The material was considered suitable and satisfactory for the purpose.

The silt (defined as finely divided solids in the contract) was transported from the settling basin in dump trucks, averaging 10 cubic yards per load, to the fire site, where it was flushed into the underground openings and voids. For all of these operations, namely loading the silt from the settling basin onto trucks, transporting it to the site, and flushing, the contractor was paid 52 cents per cubic yard for 56,720 cubic yards, at a cost of $29,494.40. At this point in the operations the supply of suitable silt material became exhausted in the previously designated settling basin and it became necessary to procure this material from a new location approximately 1 mile more distant from operations, which required trucking over adverse grades and road conditions. Because of the changed conditions for obtaining this material on the part of the contractor, it was necessary to negotiate a change order to the contract which called for increasing the unit price from 52 cents to 62 cents per cubic yard. This addition to the contract is covered by change order No. 2, a copy of which is appended.

Under this change order, 24,805 cubic yards of material was used in connection with the flushing and sealing operations until the end of the project on February 15, 1952. This material, at 62 cents per cubic yard, cost $15,379.10.

Table 1, appended, shows the number and depth of the boreholes, the quantity of silt flushed into the boreholes drilled by both the Government and the Hudson Coal Company, and the holes equipped with just thermocouples or thermocouples and air sampling tubes. Among other things, this table shows that there was a minimum of 4 cubic yards and a maximum of 5,490 cubic yards, or an average of 471 cubic yards, flushed into each borehole.

Flushing Method Used

The flushing method used consisted of either dumping a quantity of silt into the ejector box, as shown in appended photograph No. 75026, or where conditions were suitable dumping it on the ground over the borehole as shown in appended photograph No. 75018. In the case of the ejector box a coarse metal screen was used to prevent large pieces of foreign matter entering and blocking the borehole. In the case of the silt dumped on the ground, a perforated metal box was used for this purpose.

Two streams of water were used to slurry the silt material and flush it into the boreholes. Appended photographs Nos. 75018 and 75026 show one stream of water. The other stream is located down near the borehole in photograph No. 75018 and is installed in the bottom of the ejector box in photograph No. 75026.

It was found by experimentation that about 35 percent solid material to 65 percent liquid matter was the most suitable material mixture to be flushed in the boreholes. Mixtures with a higher percentage of solid frequently clogged and blocked the hole from further silting operations. Under these conditions and other conditions, such as caving of the walls of the boreholes, it was necessary to reopen holes by drilling.

In connection with determining the most suitable mixture, a water meter was provided and the volume of silt was determined. In order to determine the percentage of silt by volume the following formula was used:

$$\frac{\text{Gallons of } H_2O}{7.48 \times 27} = \text{cubic yards of } H_2O$$

$$\frac{\text{Cubic yards silt} \times 100}{\text{Cubic yards silt} + \text{cubic yards } H_2O} = \text{percentage of silt by volume}$$

All the boreholes flushed were flushed to refusal. Where loose and broken ground was encountered the casing pipe was raised several feet and cut off level with the ground and then additional flushing operations were attempted. This was repeated until all of the casing was salvaged from the boreholes. In most cases after raising the casing, a large quantity of silt was again flushed in the hole.

Salvaging Casing Pipe

Two methods were employed in salvaging casing pipe from boreholes. The first method consisted of placing a steel bar through holes burned in opposite sides of the casing, and the pipe was removed from the borehole, where feasible, by jacking.

The second method was to lift the pipe with the angledozer blade; appended photograph No. 77425 shows the angledozer being used for this purpose.

Angledozing

In accordance with the specification, the surface area within the heavy boundary lines shown on Exhibit A, appended, was graded, leveled, and filled to relatively even contours and easy grades by angledozing. An angledozer was also used for making and maintaining roads and removing fences, hedge rows, and trees, all in the vicinity of the borehole sites, as called for in change order No. 3. For this work, 1,011 angledozer hours was used; at $7.00 per hour this cost $7,077.00.

Temperature Readings and Gas Testing

Personnel of the Bureau of Mines installed thermocouples or thermocouples and tubing in 26 boreholes for taking periodic temperature readings and collecting air samples. Drawing S-334, appended, shows the details of this installation.

Appended photograph No. 75028 shows equipment used in this work and a temperature reading being taken.

Prior to and during the time fire control operations were being carried on, carbon monoxide and deficient oxygen atmospheres were encountered in the basement of a number of the homes in the fire area. The carbon monoxide content of this atmosphere, as obtained on a carbon monoxide indicating detector, was as much as 0.1 of 1 percent. Furnace fires were frequently extinguished by these gases, and at least two small domesticated animals were killed. Since this condition was of much concern to those prosecuting the control work and especially to local residents, it was necessary to install ventilating fans in a number of the basements and provide the residents with some facilities for detecting oxygen deficient atmospheres; appended photograph No. 75024 shows a resident testing for oxygen deficient atmospheres in the basement of a home in the affected area.

Restoration

A form of release, prepared by personnel of the Government and approved by officials of the Hudson Coal Company and the City of Carbondale, was signed by the property owners. The release, copy appended, relieves the Government, its agents, contractors, subcontractors, and those working with it of certain stated responsibilities. It does provide, however, "That upon completion of the work the said Government of the United States shall restore the surface of the land to substantially its original level and contour and shall restore or replace any outbuildings, fences, hedges, fruit or other trees, which may have been removed or damaged in the course of the work."

Owing to the necessity of providing roads for operating heavy machinery and trucks on lawns and small truck gardens, 4,840 cubic yards of top soil was required to restore the surface of the land to substantially its original level and contour. Also in these operations it was necessary to remove fences, hedge rows, and trees. Moreover, after work was completed in a given area, road building materials and spilled flushing material had to be removed before the top soil was applied. To conduct these operations, it was necessary to negotiate change order No. 3, copy appended. The 4,840 cubic yards of top soil used, known in the change order as borrowed noncombustible back fill material, cost 62 cents per cubic yard, for a total cost of $3,000.80. A total of 2,806 hours of laborers' services was necessary to do the restoration work; at $2.00 an hour this work cost $5,612.00. In connection with the restoration work, it was necessary to procure fencing materials, as covered in change order No. 4 copy appended. The fencing material, which cost $1,588.16, included the following:

13 rolls woven wire lawn fence at $16.84 per roll	$ 218.92
310 fence posts, cherry wood, at $1.20 each	372.00
2,500 fence pickets, wood, at 15 cents each	375.00
355 2" x 4" x 16' fence rails at $1.707 per length	605.99
50# 20d spikes at 10 cents per pound	5.00
50# 10d nails at 9 cents per pound	4.50
25# 6d nails at 8 cents per pound	2.00
25# 1d staples at 19 cents per pound	4.75
Total	$1,588.16

Photograph No. 77428 appended shows laborers constructing fences in the area where fences had previously been removed during the course of drilling and flushing operations. Photographs Nos. 77429 and 77430 appended show some of the completed fences and areas where the surface had been restored by the addition of top soil. Photograph No. 77431 appended shows part of the area on which top soil has been applied and angledozed to relatively even grades and contour.

MISCELLANEOUS

In the prosecution of the work in connection with the control of this fire, it was necessary to purchase additional material and supplies, such as thermocouple wire, copper tubing fittings, copper tubing, an ejector bin, and a vacuum air pump for collecting air samples; the cost of these materials and supplies was $997.71. In addition, material for the construction of roads and the rental of equipment for this purpose cost $879.00.

One of the two ejector bins previously mentioned as used in connection with the control work was purchased by the Government; the other ejector bin was furnished gratis by the contractor.

WORK DONE BY THE HUDSON COAL COMPANY

Work done by the Hudson Coal Company, in accordance with the agreement previously mentioned and appended, consisted of stripping the overburden from the burning coal beds and removing it from the site. As previously mentioned in this report, the Hudson Coal Company is continuing this work.

Appended photograph No. 75021 shows burning carbonaceous materials along the highwall of the strip pit, and appended photographs Nos. 75023, 75027, and 73912 show some of the equipment being operated to remove the overburden and burning carbonaceous material.

COST OF THE PROJECT

The following tabulation shows the total cost of this fire control project:

Churn drilling	$ 24,920.30
New casing	5,878.00
Installing casing	2,034.50
Salvaging casing	126.00
Capping	66.00
Flushing	44,873.50
Angledozing	7,077.00
Restoration work	10,200.96
	95,176.26
Instrumentation of boreholes, other purchases, etc.	1,876.71
	97,052.97
10 percent for supervision and administration	9,705.29
Total cost to Government as of February 15, 1952	106,758.26
Expenditures by Hudson Coal Company through July 15, 1950, for which credit has been allowed	214,071.64
Total cost of project	$ 320,829.90

LETTERS OF COMMENDATION

The Regional Director, Mr. H. P. Greenwald, received two letters commending the Bureau on the work of controlling this fire. One of the letters is from Mr. E. C. Weichel, vice president of the Hudson Coal Company, copy appended, and the other is from the Mayor of the City of Carbondale, Mr. Walter J. Brydon, copy appended. These letters convey expressions of satisfaction on the manner in which work on the project was conducted.

CONCLUSION

After flushing 81,525 cubic yards of silt into the underground voids in the mine fire area, it appears reasonably certain that a seal has been established and the fire has been brought under control. In addition to excluding air from the fire area, it is believed that the filling of the underground voids will stabilize the ground and minimize further subsidence. The filling of all crevices and cracks of the surface with the incombustible silt material and maintaining the seal will prevent the emission of fumes and gases. Much of the difficulty previously encountered with gases entering basements of homes in the vicinity has cleared up, and it is expected that this condition will improve in other homes that are now being affected.

ACKNOWLEDGMENT

The many courtesies extended and assistance given by the officials of the Hudson Coal Company, the City of Carbondale, and others are gratefully acknowledged.

Respectfully submitted,

F. E. Griffith

F. E. Griffith
Mining Engineer

E. P. Thomas

E. P. Thomas
Resident Engineer

Approved by:

James Westfield

James Westfield, Chief
Accident Prevention and
Health Division, Region VIII

COMMONWEALTH OF PENNSYLVANIA
DEPARTMENT OF MINES

Pottsville, Penna.
April 5, 1954

Honorable W. J. Clements
Secretary of Mines
Harrisburg, Penna.

Dear Mr. Clements:

Attached hereto is a complete statement of the work accomplished by Harvey B. Moyer, Inc., at the Carbondale Mine Fire, for the month of March, 1954. Included are bore hole records, flushing records, and statement of extraneous work, together with the totals.

The details of the statement are as follows:

Total bore hole footage drilled	2606
Total flushing material placed - cubic yards	8264
Bulldozer	1 hour
Bore holes capped	3

A total of 107 feet 8 inches of casing is tied up in holes presently capped. However I do not believe this should be paid for at this time because future developments may require that we flush these holes, at which time the contractor can salvage the casing if he so desires. I recommend that no casing be paid for until the final estimate on this job.

Yours very truly,

Gordon E. Smith
Deputy Secretary of Mines

GES:lel
encl.

NOTES

Introduction

[1] Henry Lee, "Town on a Hot Seat," *Pageant*, July 1957, 70–77.

Chapter 1: Mine Fires

[1] Kevin Krajick, "Fire in the Hole," *Smithsonian*, May 2005, available online at www.smithsonianmag.com/travel/firehole.html.

[2] F. E. Griffith, M. O. Magnuson, and G. J. R. Toothman, *Control of Fires in Inactive Coal Formations in the United States* (Washington, DC: United States Government Printing Office, Bulletin 590, 1060), 3.

[3] Ibid. Another reference to this fire was found in the diary of David McClure, found by the author in Howard N. Eavenson, "The Pittsburgh Coal Bed—Its Early History and Development," *Transaction of AIME, Coal Division* 130 (1938): 9–10.

[4] Ibid.

[5] Ibid. No date is given for its conclusion.

[6] Ibid.

[7] Ibid.

[8] U.S. Department of the Interior Bureau of Mines, *Three Mine Fire Control Projects in Northeastern Pennsylvania* (Washington, DC: U.S. Government Printing Office, 1971), 2.

[9] Interview with Michael C. Korb, P.E., Environmental Program Manager, Bureau of Abandoned Mine Reclamation, Department of Environmental Protection, Commonwealth of Pennsylvania, January 15, 2009. Mr. Korb reviewed this section and added some significant insights to it, as noted throughout.

[10] Ibid.

[11] Ibid.

[12] Griffith et al., 10.

[13] Ibid.

[14] Ibid.

[15] Ibid.

[16] Krajick, "Fire in the Hole."

[17] Griffith et al., 10–11.

[18] Ibid. According to the authors, similar situations are thought to occur in strip mines and mine-refuse dumps, but this may not be the case. Burning mine refuse dumps are most often thought to be ignited by outside sources. Likewise, strip-mine fires are not often found to be the result of an external fire igniting the combustibles within the pile.

[19] Robert F. Chaiken, Robert J. Brennan, Bernice S. Heisey, Ann G. Kim, Wilbert T. Malenka, and John T. Schimmel, *Problems in the Control of Anthracite Mine Fires: A Case Study of the Centralia Mine Fire* (Avondale, MD: U.S. Department of the Interior, Bureau of Mines, 1983), 16–18.

[20] Krajick, "Fire in the Hole."

[21] Griffith et al., 18–44.

[22] Ibid.

[23] Ibid.

[24] Korb.

[25] Chaiken et al., *A Case Study*, 16.

[26] Ibid.

[27] Ibid.

[28] Ibid, 17.

[29] Korb, January 15, 2009.

[30] Chaiken et al., *A Case Study*, 18.

[31] Ibid.

[32] Ibid., 15.

[33] Ibid., 15–18.

[34] Ibid.

[35] Ibid., 19–20, 36, 40–42. Studies clearly point to the fact that complete excavation of the fire is the one approach that has a high probability of success. See also an earlier study: G. E. McElroy, *Some Observations on the Causes, Behavior, and Control of Fires in Steep-Pitch Anthracite Mines*, U.S. Bureau of Mines, IC 7025, 1938. It is interesting to note that the materials available for eradication of mine fires found in Federal Bureau of Mines sources have not changed for many years, presumably indicating that these approaches remain the most common ones used today.

[36] Chaiken et al., *A Case Study*, 20. See also G. E. McElroy, *Some Observations*, cited immediately above.

[37] Korb.

Chapter 2: Carbondale, The Pioneer City

[1] H. M. D. Hollister, *History of the Lackawanna Valley* (Philadelphia: J. B. Lippincott, 1885). 295-300. Thomas Murphy, *Jubilee History of Lackawanna County, Pennsylvania* (Topeka, KS: Historical Publishing Company, 1928), 428–449.

[2] Hollister, *History of the Lackawanna Valley*, 295–300. Murphy, *Jubilee History*, 428–33.

[3] Murphy, *Jubilee History*, 428–33. See also Cheryl A. Kashuba, "Carbondale: Coal Country," *The Sunday Times*, August 3, 2008, D1.

[4] Hollister, *History of the Lackawanna Valley*, 295–300.

[5] Murphy, *Jubilee History*, 429.

[6] Ibid.

[7] Kashuba, "Carbondale: Coal Country."

[8] Ibid.

[9] Steward Pearce, *Annals of Luzerne County* (Philadelphia: J. P. Lippincott, 1860), 182.

[10] Temple University, "An Economic Rehabilitation Proposal for the Northeast Industrial Area of Pennsylvania," *Pennsylvania's Mineral Heritage*, Summaries 1–4, 1944.

[11] Ibid.

[12] Thomas Hannon, "A Geographical Analysis of Population Trends in Lackawanna County, Pennsylvania," M.S. thesis, Pennsylvania State University, 1956, 48–49.

[13] Temple University.

[14] Ibid.

[15] As reported in *The Congressional Record, Senate*, February 20, 1956, p. 2479. Mayor Kelly's statement was made before a subcommittee on Labor and Public Service of the U.S. Senate hearing on unemployment on February 10, 1956 in Wilkes-Barre, Pennsylvania.

[16] Information on Carbondale was drawn by the author from various historical sources. Contributing to this section: Mary M. Purcell and William J. Purcell, longtime Carbondale natives and residents. Interviews conducted in 2009. Ms. Purcell recalled that during its mining and railroad days, Carbondale was essentially a "blue-collar town." The various industrial jobs were for males only, except for a few positions filled by females in the administration offices of the firms. The male workers, said Purcell, were represented by two powerful unions—the mines by the United Mine Workers of America (UMWA), the railroad men by the "Brotherhoods." Each railroad union, such as The Brotherhood of Firemen and Engineers, represented a specific employee group. Purcell recalled further that it was interesting to note that workers of this era had a very real devotion to their particular union. "Indeed," she wrote, "the railroad men regarded the 'Brotherhood' of their union in a very special way." This was true also of miners and the United Mine

Workers Union. Mining, she noted, forged a special relationship among the men who worked underground and far from outside help in an emergency. They actually depended on each other for their lives. Every miner and laborer was trained in first aid, a program of immediate medical assistance to be given in an emergency—invented by a native of Jermyn, Pennsylvania—that could mean the difference between life and death in a mining accident. Local textile workers were likewise represented by a powerful union, the International Ladies Garment Workers Union (ILGWU) that in its heyday maintained a resort (Unity House) for its members in the Pocono Mountains. Others who contributed were those who were interviewed specifically about the mine fire; they are cited in later footnotes.

CHAPTER 3: THE UNDERGROUND INFERNO

[1] Charles Remsberg, "The Fire That's Saving a Small Town," *The Kiwanis Magazine*, June 1965, 27–31, 46–47.

[2] "Summary, Carbondale Mine Fire Control Project," *U.S. Department of the Interior, Bureau of Mines, Report: Proposed Carbondale Mine Fire Control Project,* U.S. Department of Surface Mining, Wilkes-Barre, PA, undated.

[3] Interviews with Jack Gillen, Joseph McGraw, and Jack Teeple, 1998. There are differing views about who or what caused the trash to ignite. But there is general agreement that the mine fire started as a result of burning trash at the dump site.

[4] "Fire Under the Streets," *Time*, August 1, 1956.

[5] Interviews with Mary Purcell, Helen Kane, and Catherine Kane, 1997–98.

[6] C. P. Gilmore, "A City on Fire," *The Saturday Evening Post*, September 7, 1963, 85. See also Bob Tomaine, "Still Burning Mine Fire Drove Out 1,000," *The Sunday Times*, February 23, 1997, A1, A11.

[7] Interviews with Mary Purcell, Dr. Thomas Coleman, Attorney Joseph McGraw, and Catherine and Helen Kane, 1997–98.

[8] Catherine and Helen Kane interview, 1998.

[9] Ibid. Also, Mary Purcell, 1997.

[10] Lee, "Town on a Hot Seat," 74.

[11] Remsberg, "The Fire That's Saving a Small Town," 29. Jack Gillen talks about these processes in his interview, 1998.

[12] Lee, "Town on a Hot Seat," 74–75. The drilling and flushing project into the workings of the Hudson Coal Company, where the mine fire burned in 1950 and 1951, was supervised by the Federal Bureau of Mines. The Federal Bureau also supervised the placing of inert materials over the surface area. After a "considerable amount" of work was done, the Bureau reported to the mayor of Carbondale, William Monahan, that the fire was out. A report by Pennsylvania Mine Inspector James F. Munley to the Pennsylvania Department of Mines, in the "Carbondale Mine Fire" file, Pennsylvania State Archives, Pennsylvania Historical and Museum Commission, Harrisburg, PA, undated.

[13] Gilmore, "A City on Fire," 85. The Collins deaths became part of a report submitted by James F. Munley, State Mine Inspector for the First District to his superiors at the State Bureau of Mines in Harrisburg. In this report, Mr. Munley described the tragedy, saying that James Collins had gone to his aunt and uncle's home because the couple had not been seen for some time. There was no response to his calls and knocking, so he entered the house and found the bodies in their bedroom. One window in the room was raised about three-and-a-half inches. Mr. Collins and neighbors then called Francis Judge, the Carbondale Chief of Police, who called Dr. Charles Speicher, Deputy Coroner of Lackawanna County. The coroner made his investigation and ascertained that the Collins couple had been dead about eighteen hours prior to the discovery of their bodies. Hudson Coal Company officials and E. C. McCleary, Area Engineer of the Federal Bureau of Mines were notified of the deaths. The Hudson Coal Company and the Federal Bureau were in charge of the drilling operations. Subsequent investigation disclosed that there was .02% carbon monoxide in the bedroom where the bodies were found and comparable amounts in other parts of the home. Munley Report to the Pennsylvania Bureau of Mines, 1952, in the "Carbondale Mine Fire" file, Pennsylvania State Archives, Pennsylvania Historical and Museum Commission, Harrisburg, PA.

[14] Gilmore, "A City on Fire," 85.

[15] Interview with Dr. Thomas Coleman, 1997. Mr. and Mrs. Collins were his patients, and he confirmed the results of the medical examination in his interview with the author in 1998.

[16] Several members of the Purcell–Cooper family were nearly killed as a result of carbon monoxide seepage into their homes on 57 South Hospital Street early on a Sunday morning. They were saved because they had awakened early to prepare to attend Mass. Interview with Mary Purcell, 1998.

[17] Gilmore, "A City on Fire," 85.

[18] Ibid.

[19] Interview with Edward Spall, questionnaire, August 29, 2008.

[20] Ibid.

[21] Interview with Mary Louise Germano Nepa, June 24, 2008.

[22] Ibid.

[23] U.S. Department of Interior, Bureau of Mines, "Summary, Carbondale Mine Fire Control Project," Report: Proposed Mine Fire Control Project, Wilkes-Barre, PA, undated.

[24] Conversation with William J. Cooper, 1960.

[25] Remsberg, "The Fire That's Saving a Small Town," 28. A more recent article on mine fires in Northeastern Pennsylvania's anthracite coal region details at least five mine fires in the northern coal fields. See Tomaine, 1997, A10.

[26] Gilmore, "A City on Fire," 85.

[27] Martin Campbell, quoted in Gilmore, "A City on Fire," 85.

[28] Tomaine, "Still Burning Mine Fire Drove Out 1,000," A11.

[29] Mary Louise Germano Nepa interview, 2008.

[30] Spall questionnaire, 2008.

[31] Interview with Rosemary Tryon Grizzanti, June 10, 2008.

[32] Gilmore, "A City on Fire," p. 85.

[33] Quoted in Remsberg, "The Fire That's Saving a Small Town," 30.

[34] Grizzanti interview.

[35] Interview with Dr. Coleman. Also, interviews with Mrs. Costanzo and Mrs. Bonacci, 1998.

[36] Gilmore, "A City on Fire," 85.

[37] Ibid.

[38] Quoted in Lee, "Town on a Hot Seat," 71.

[39] Gilmore, "A City on Fire," 72.

[40] Ibid. See also Lee, "Town on a Hot Seat," 77, for quote using this term by *The Carbondale Daily News* editor, Tom Gilmartin.

[41] Remsberg, "The Fire That's Saving a Small Town," 30.

CHAPTER 4: THE BIG DIG-OUT PROJECT

[1] Remsberg, "The Fire That's Saving a Small Town," 30. See also Lee, "Town on a Hot Seat," 73–74.

[2] Leo Coleman, quoted in Gilmore, "A City on Fire," 85.

[3] Ibid.

[4] Gilmore, "A City on Fire," 85.

[5] Stanley Cominsky, quoted in Gilmore, "A City on Fire," 85.

[6] Ibid.

[7] Ibid.

[8] Grizzanti interview.

[9] John Gilroy, quoted in Lee, "Town on a Hot Seat," 76.

[10] Lee, "Town on a Hot Seat," 72.

[11] Perri, quoted in Gilmore, "A City on Fire," 85.

[12] Lee, "Town on a Hot Seat," 72. U.S. Dept. of the Interior, Bureau of Mines, "Summary: Carbondale Mine Fire Control Project." Following the deaths of Patrick and Elizabeth Collins in 1952, Mayor Frank Kelly acted aggressively and declared an emergency. Two years earlier, the Pennsylvania Department of Mines had conducted a meeting in Harrisburg to address Carbondale's plight. At this meeting, state mine inspectors and representatives of the U.S. Department of Mines formulated the initial plan of attack—a cooperative agreement between the Hudson Coal Company and the United States acting through the Department of the Interior, Bureau of Mines, dated May 25, 1950. This plan, a joint state–federal effort to

control the fire, had involved the flushing operation referred to earlier. The Bureau of Mines estimated that it would cost $54,515. The coal company was credited with expenditures of $175,412 to the date of this plan and by February 26, 1953, a total contribution of $214,071.61. The Bureau continued to spend money on this project until 1956 (May 18), for a total of $256,512.35. It was called "control work."

[13] U.S. Dept. of the Interior, Bureau of Mines, "Summary: Carbondale Mine Fire Control Project."

[14] Ibid. The city, located at six hundred feet, was higher than the surrounding region, and draining the lakes would send water flowing into mines under communities at lower altitudes than Carbondale.

[15] Ibid.

[16] Gilmartin, quoted in Remsberg, "The Fire That's Saving a Small Town," 31.

[17] Lee, "Town on a Hot Seat," 75.

[18] Mayor Kelly, quoted in Remsberg, "The Fire That's Saving a Small Town," 31.

[19] *The Carbondale Daily News*, April 24, 1954, n.p.

[20] Lee, "Town on a Hot Seat," 75–76. Mayor Kelly, a Democrat, supported Congressman Carrigg, a Republican, when he ran for reelection.

[21] David Walker, quoted in Lee, "Town on a Hot Seat," 76.

[22] Interview with Bernard Blier, 1998.

[23] Ibid.

[24] Robert W. Bell, quoted in *Time*, August 10, 1956. According to Jack Gillen, an owner of Gillen Coal Company, interviewed in 2010, Hudson Coal Company had started the Carbondale Coal Company as a subsidiary in order to defer their liability since Hudson Coal was the major regional monopoly on the land and coal. Gillen Coal and De Weise Coal were two local coal companies involved in stripping. Then Gillen Coal and De Weise Coal "received contracts to help the Carbondale Coal Company with the fire and to take out the coal. It was agreed to sell the dirty coal to Hudson and the city as some compensation for working on a very

precise and voluminous project with innately painstaking and dangerous requirements." De Weise left and Gillen Coal took over that company as well as the Carbondale Coal Company. Eventually Carbondale Coal took Hudson, which had become Glenn Alden Coal. Jack Gillen Interview, August 27, 2010 and Candace Gillen notes, September 5 and 6, 2010.

[25] Interview, about financial arrangements, with Bernard Blier.

[26] Gilmore, "A City on Fire," 86.

[27] Martin Mann, "Inferno Under a City: Fighting the Fire That Won't Go Out," *Popular Science Monthly*, May 1960, 61. Mann said that even with a declining market for anthracite, the coal was worth in excess of $13.6 million.

[28] Gilmore, "A City on Fire." Also in Mann "Inferno Under a City: Fighting the Fire That Won't Go Out" (see note, just above).

[29] "Carbondale's Mine Fire," *The Scranton Tribune*, n.d., n.p.

[30] Ibid.

[31] Gilmore, "A City on Fire," 86.

[32] Ibid.

[33] Interview with Mary Purcell, 1997.

[34] Interview with Mrs. Gabriel (Helen) Costanzo, 1998.

[35] Interview with Louis Sirianni, 1998.

[36] Interview with Edward Spall, September 22, 2008.

[37] Interview with Mrs. Gabriel (Helen) Costanzo, 1998.

[38] Conversations with Mrs. Madeline Purcell, 1960s and 1970s.

[39] Ibid.

[40] Mrs. Purcell noted that, at the time, her brother, a retired miner with years of experience in the mines that included setting blasting charges, maintained that the amounts of blasting powder being used and the proximity of the blast to homes and people was beyond the prescribed limits. Many people complained of this to

Carbondale authorities, but nothing was ever done to address this concern. A number of former residents interviewed for this study maintained that the excessive charges were deliberate—that this was a way to hurry the residents out of their homes more quickly, to get them to sell and move on.

[41] Ibid.

[42] Ibid.

[43] Interviews with Mrs. Rosemary Tryon Grizzanti, 2008–2009.

[44] Conversation with Mrs. Grizzanti, March 2, 2009. In a separate interview with Mrs. Costanzo, she said she had written to Robert Kennedy, then Attorney General of the United States, to make him aware of the plight of people in the mine fire and, according to them, the inhuman way they were being treated by the authorities involved. Interview with Mr. and Mrs. Gabriel Costanzo, 1998.

[45] Interview with Andrew Cerra, 1997.

[46] Interview with Helen and Catherine Kane, 1998.

[47] Conversations with William Cooper, 1960.

[48] Communication from John Baldi, University of Scranton, 1997, Professor Emeritus. Baldi's study focused on determining demographic data as well as housing plans of affected families. It was requested by the federal government under the urban renewal plan and used by the Carbondale Redevelopment Authority.

[49] Interviews with Mary Purcell, Gabriel Costanzo, and Michael Bonacci, 1998.

[50]. Interviews with Helen and Catherine Kane, Michael Bonacci, Gabriel Costanzo, et al.

[51] Interview with Mary Purcell.

[52] Gilmore, "A City on Fire," 86.

[53] Mrs. Jennie Fortuner, quoted in Gilmore, "A City on Fire," 86.

[54] William Cooper, quoted in Gilmore, "A City on Fire," 87.

[55] Joseph Cerra, quoted in Gilmore, "A City on Fire," 87.

[56] Jim Collins, quoted in Gilmore, "A City on Fire," 87.

[57] Mrs. Santo Perri, quoted in Gilmore, "A City on Fire," 87.

[58] Mann, "Inferno Under a City: Fighting the Fire That Won't Go Out," 61–62, 228.

[59] Gilmore, "A City on Fire," 86. Quote is attributed to Frank Olshefski, a strip-mine worker for thirty years.

[60] Mann, "Inferno Under a City: Fighting the Fire That Won't Go Out."

[61] Ibid.

[62] Ibid.

[63] Gilmore, "A City on Fire," 86.

[64] Ibid.

[65] Interviews with Michael Bonacci, Angelo Mazza, and Gabriel Costanzo, 1997–98.

[66] Interview with Bernard Blier, 1998. Interviews with Jack Gillen, 1998 and 2010. West Side Mine Fire Files, U.S. Bureau of Surface Mining, Wilkes-Barre, PA, 1998.

[67] Gilmore, "A City on Fire," 86.

[68] Ibid. Mayor Howard had succeeded Mayor Kelly in 1960.

[69] Gilmore, "A City on Fire," 86.

[70] Lee, "Town on a Hot Seat," 72–73.

Chapter 5: Gone, But Not Forgotten

[1] "Official Report on the Carbondale Mine Fire," U.S. Bureau of Surface Mining, Wilkes-Barre, PA, n.d.

[2] *PAHRA News*, April 1972, p. 4.

[3] Ibid.

[4] Ibid.

[5] Gilmore, "A City on Fire," 87.

[6] Joseph Farrell, quoted in Gilmore, "A City on Fire," 87.

[7] Mayor Frank Howard, quoted in Gilmore, "A City on Fire," 87.

[8] Interview with Joseph McGraw, Esq., 1998. The same view is expressed by Michael Teeple, 1998.

[9] McGraw interview.

[10] Interviews with Helen and Catherine Kane, Michael Bonacci, Gabriel Costanzo, et al., 1998.

[11] Interviews with Michael Bonacci, Mr. and Mrs. Gabriel Costanzo, Mary Purcell, and Angelo Mazza, 1997–98.

[12] Grizzanti interview, 2008.

[13] Mary Purcell interview.

[14] Helen Costanzo interview.

[15] Grizzanti interview.

Bibliography

Baldi, John, Professor emeritus, University of Scranton. "Report on Carbondale Mine Fire Residents." Provided to author, 1997.

Baum, Willa K. *Oral History for the Local Historical Society*. 3rd ed., rev. Walnut Creek, CA: AltaMira, 1995.

———. *Transcribing and Editing Oral History*. Nashville, TN: American Association of State and Local History, 1977.

Bell, Robert W. Interviewed in *Time*, August 10, 1956.

Blier, Bernard. Interviewed by the author, Nov 14, 1997.

Bodnar, John. *Anthracite People*. Harrisburg, PA: Pennsylvania Historical and Museum Commission, 1983.

Bogart, Barbara Allen, and William Lynwood Montell. *From Memory to History: Using Oral Sources for Historical Research*. Nashville, TN: American Association for State and Local History, 1981.

Bonacci, Mr. and Mrs.Michael (Mary). Interviewed by the author, June 18, 1998.

Bonacci, Theresa and Antoinette (daughters of Michael and Mary Bonacci). Interviewed by the author, July 21, 1998.

"Carbondale's Mine Fire." *The Scranton Tribune*. Undated clipping, n.p.

"Carbondale, Pa. West Side Mine Fire Area." Available online at www.italygenes.com/minefire/carbondale.html.

Carroll, Richard Patrick. Completed a questionnaire for the author, November 22, 2009.

Cerra, Andrew. Interviewed by the author, August 14, 1997.

Cerra, Joseph. Interviewed by C. P. Gilmore, "A City on Fire." *The Saturday Evening Post*, September 7, 1963.

Coleman, Leo. Interviewed by C. P. Gilmore, "A City on Fire." *The Saturday Evening Post*, September 7, 1963.

Coleman, Thomas. Interviewed by the author, December 16, 1997.

Collins, James. Interviewed by C. P. Gilmore, "A City on Fire." *The Saturday Evening Post*, September 7, 1963, p. 87.

Cominsky, Stanley. Interviewed by C. P. Gilmore, "A City on Fire." *The Saturday Evening Post*, September 7, 1963, p. 85.

Cooper, William. Interviewed by C. P. Gilmore, "A City on Fire." *The Saturday Evening Post*, September 7, 1963, p. 85. Conversations with author, 1960s.

Costanzo, Mr. and Mrs. Gabriel. Interviewed by the author, June 23, 1998.

Devers, Maureen. Interviewed by the author, August 8, 1997.

Davis, Cullom, Kathryn Black, and Kay McLean. *Oral History: From Tape to Type*. Chicago, IL: American Library Association, 1977.

Dunaway, David K., and Willa K. Baum, ed. *Oral History: An Interdisciplinary Anthology*, 2nd ed. Walnut Creek, CA: AltaMira, 1996.

Everett, Stephen E. *Oral History Techniques and Procedures*. Washington, DC: Center of Military History, United States Army, 1992. Available online at http://www.army.mil/cmh-pg/books/oral.htm.

Eavenson, Howard N. "The Pittsburgh Coal Bed—Its Early History and Development." *Transaction AIME, Coal Division* 130 (1938): pp. 9–10.

"Fire Under the Streets." *Time*, August 10, 1959. Available online at www.time.com/time/magazine/article/09171,611233-2,001.htm.

Farrell, Joseph. Interviewed by C. P. Gilmore, "A City on Fire." *The Saturday Evening Post*, September 7, 1963, p. 87.

Fletcher, William. *Recording Your Family History: A Guide to Preserving Oral History with Video Tape, Audio Tape, Suggested Topics and Questions*. New York: Dodd, Mead, 1986.

Fortuner, Jennie. Interviewed by C. P. Gilmore, "A City on Fire." *The Saturday Evening Post*, September 7, 1963, p. 86.

Frank, Benis M. *A "Do-It-Yourself" Oral History Primer*. Washington, DC: History and Museums Division, Headquarters, U.S. Marine Corps, 1982.

Gilmartin, Thomas. Interviewed by Henry Lee, "Town on a Hot Seat." *Pageant*, July, 1957, p. 77.

Gilroy, John. Interviewed by Henry Lee, "Town on a Hot Seat." *Pageant*, July, 1957, p. 76.

Gillen, Candace. Written comments, September 5 and 6, 2010.

Gillen, Jack. Interviewed by the author, January 9, 1998, and August 27, 2010.

Griffith, F. E., M. O. Magnuson, and G. J. R. Toothman. *Control of Fires in Inactive Coal Formations in the United States*. Washington, DC: U.S. Government Printing Office, 1960, p. 3._

Grizzanti, Rosemary Tryon. Interviewed by the author, June 10, 2008.

Hannon, Thomas. "A Geographical Anlysis of Population Trends in Lackawanna County, Pennsylvania." M.S. thesis, Pennsylvania State University, 1965, 48–49.

Havlice, Patricia Pate. *Oral History: A Reference Guide and Annotated Bibliography*. Jefferson, NC: McFarland, 1985.

Hollister, H. M. D. *History of the Lackawanna Valley*, 3rd ed. Philadelphia: J. B. Lippincott, 1885, pp. 1–154.

Hoopes, James. *Oral History: An Introduction for Students*. Chapel Hill: University of North Carolina Press, 1979.

Howard, Frank, Mayor of Carbondale. Interviewed by C. P. Gilmore, "A City on Fire." *The Saturday Evening Post*, September 7, 1963, p. 87.

Hsieh-Yee, Ingrid. *Organizing Audiovisual and Electronic Resources for Access: A Cataloging Guide*. Englewood, CO: Libraries Unlimited, 2000.

Ives, Edward D. *The Tape-Recorded Interview*. Knoxville: University of Tennessee, 1980.

Jackson, Bruce. *Fieldwork*. Urbana: University of Illinois Press, 1987.

James, Ann Morrison. Completed a questionnaire for the author, September 11, 2008.

Kashuba, Cheryl. "Carbondale Coal Country." *The Sunday Times*, August 3, 2008, p. D1G

Kane, Catherine. Interviewed by the author, January 24, 1998.

Kane, Helen. Interviewed by the author, January 24, 1998.

Kelly, Frank, Mayor of Carbondale. Quoted in the *Congressional Record: Senate*, February 20, 1956.

Kelly, Mrs. Frank. Interviewed by the author, December 6, 1997.

Korb, Michael C., P.E., Environmental Program Manager, Bureau of Abandoned Mine Reclamation, Department of Environmental Protection, Commonwealth of Pennsylvania. Information provided to the author, January 15, 2009.

Krajick, Kevin. "Fire in the Hole." *Smithsonian*, May 2005. Available online at www.smithsonianmag.com/travel/firehole.html.

Kroll-Smith, Stephen, and Stephen Robert Couch. *The Real Disaster is Above Ground: A Mine Fire and Social Conflict*. Lexington: University of Kentucky, 1990.

Kress, Leonard. *The Centralia Mine Fire*. St. Chico, CA: Flume, 1987.

Lance, David. *An Archive Approach to Oral History*. London: Imperial War Museum, 1978.

Lee, Henry. "Town on a Hot Seat." *Pageant*. July 1957, pp. 70–77.

Mann, Martin. "Inferno Under a City: Fighting the Fire That Won't Go Out." *Popular Science Monthly*, May 1960, pp. 59–63, 223–28.

Matters, Marion. *Oral History Cataloging Manual*. Chicago, IL: Society of American Archivists, 1995.

Mazza, Angelo. Interviewed by the author, June 24, 1998.

McClure, David, found by the authors in Howard N. Eavenson, "The Pittsburgh Coal Bed—Its Early History and Development." *Transaction AIME, Coal division* 130 (1938): pp. 9–10.

McElroy, G. E. *Some Observations on the Causes, Behavior, and Control of Fires in Steep-Pitch Anthracite Mines*, Bureau of Mines IC 7025. 1938.

McGraw, Joseph, Esq. Interviewed by the author, November 14, 1997.

Mosley, Philip. *Anthracite: An Anthology of Pennsylvania Coal Region Plays*. Scranton, PA: University of Scranton Press, 2006.

Moss, William. *Oral History Program Manual*. New York: Praeger, 1974.

Murphy, Thomas, *Jubilee History of Lackawanna County, Pennsylvania*, Topeka, KS: Historical Publishing Company, 1928.

Nepa, Mary Louise Germano. Completed a questionnaire for the author, June 24, 2008.

Neuenschwander, John A. *Oral History and the Law*, 2nd ed., rev. Denton, TX: Oral History Association, 1993.

Oral History Association. *Oral History Evaluation Guidelines*. Carlisle, PA: Dickinson College, 1989. Available online at http://omega.dickinson.edu/organizations/oha/pub_eg.html.

Pennsylvania Department of Internal Affairs. "An Economic Rehabilitation Proposal for the Northeast Industrial Area of Pennsylvania." In *Pennsylvania Mineral Heritage Summaries*. Philadelphia, PA: Temple University, 1944, pp. 1–4.

PAHRA News, April 1972, p. 4.

Pearce, Steward. *Annals of Luzerne County*. Philadelphia, PA: J. P. Lippincott, 1860, p. 182.

Pennsylvania State University. *Historical Statistics of Pennsylvania's Mineral Industries, 1759–1955*, March 1957.

Perri, Mrs. Santo. Interviewed by C. P. Gilmore, "A City on Fire." *The Saturday Evening Post*, September 7, 1963, p. 87.

Perri, Santo. Interviewed by C. P. Gilmore, "A City on Fire." *The Saturday Evening Post*, September 7, 1963, p. 85.

Purcell, Mary. Interviewed by the author, 1997, 1998. (She also compiled historical material on Carbondale for the author, 2009.)

Purcell, William J. Compiled historical material on Carbondale for the author, 2008.

Remsberg, Charles. "The Fire That's Saving a Small Town." *Kiwanis Magazine*, June 1965, pp. 27–31, 46–47.

Ritchie, Donald A. *Doing Oral History*. New York: Twayne, 1995.

Sirianni, Louis. Interviewed by the author, July 21, 1998.

Sitton, Thad, George L. Mehaffy, and O. L. Davis, Jr. *Oral History: A Guide for Teachers (and Others)*. Austin: University of Texas Press, 1983.

Sommer, Barbara W., and Mary Kay Quinlan. "A Guide to Oral History Interviews," Technical Leaflet #210. American Association for State and Local History. Included in *History News* 55, 3 (Summer 2000).

———. *The Oral History Manual*. Walnut Creek, CA: AltaMira, 2002.

Spall, Edward. Completed a questionnaire for the author, August 22 and 29, 2008.

Stielow, Frederick J. *The Management of Oral History Sound Archives*. New York: Greenwood Press, 1986.

Teeple, Jack. Interviewed by the author, November 14, 1997.

Thompson, Paul. *The Voice of the Past: Oral History*. Oxford: Oxford University Press, 1978.

Tomaine, Bob. "Still Burning Mine Fire Drove Out 1,000." *The Sunday Times*, February 23, 1997, pp. A1, A11.

———. "Illegal Dumping Seen as Sources of Mine Fires." *The Sunday Times*, February 23, 1997, p. A10.

U.S. Department of the Interior, Bureau of Mines, Chaiken, Robert F., Robert J. Brennan, Bernice S. Heisey, Ann G. Kim, Wilbert T. Malenka, and John T. Schimmel. *Problems in the Control of Anthracite Mine Fires: A Case Study of the Centralia Mine Fire*. Washington, DC: U. S. Department of the Interior, n.d., p. 15.

U. S. Department of the Interior, Bureau of Mines, Chaiken, Robert F. *Controlled Burnout of Wasted Coal on Abandoned Coal Mine Lands*, Report of Investigations 8478. Washington, DC: U. S. Department of the Interior, 1980.

U.S. Department of the Interior, Bureau of Mines, Kim, Ann G., Thomas

R. Justin, and John F. Miller. *Mine Fire Diagnostics Applied to Carbondale, PA Mine Fire Site*, Report of Investigations 9421. Washington, DC: U.S. Department of the Interior, 1992. Available online at www. Cdc.gov/niosh/mining/pubs/pdfs/ri9421.pdf.

U.S. Department of the Interior, Bureau of Mines. *Official Report, Carbondale Mine Fire Packet*. Wilkes-Barre, PA: U.S. Department of the Interior, n.d.

U.S. Department of the Interior, Bureau of Mines. *Report: Proposed Carbondale Mine Fire Control Project*, Wilkes-Barre, PA: U.S. Department of Surface Mining, n.d.

U.S. Department of the Interior, Bureau of Mines, Dierks, H. A., R. H. Whaite, and A. H. Harvey. *Three Mine Fire Control Projects in Northeastern Pennsylvania*, Information Circular 8524. Washington, DC, 1971.

U.S. Department of the interior, Bureau of Mines, Andreuzzi, Frank C. *A Method for Extinguishing and Removing Burning Coal Refuse Banks*, Information Circular 8485. Washington, DC, 1970.

United States Holocaust Memorial Museum. *Oral History Interview Guidelines*. Washington, DC: The Museum, 1998. Available online at http://www.ushmm.org/archives/oralhist.pdf.

Walker, David. Interviewed by Henry Lee, "Town on a Hot Seat." *Pageant*, July 1957, p. 76.

Ward, Alan. *A Manual of Sound Archive Administration*. Brookfield, VT: Gower, 1990.

Whitman, Glenn. *Dialogue with the Past: Engaging Students and Meeting Standards Through Oral History*. Walnut Creek, CA: AltaMira, 2004.

Yow, Valerie Raleigh. *Recording Oral History: A Practical Guide for Social Scientists*. Thousand Oaks, CA: SAGE, 1994.